ORGANIZATIONAL COMMITMENT:
ENHANCING OF PRODUCTIVITY AND TURNOVER

MASTERING THE ART OF SUSTAINABLE BUSINESS COMPETITIVENESS

By
KELECHIKWU EMMANUEL, OGUEJIOFOR

©A Published Work in Fulfillment of the Requirement for the Award
Master of Business Administration

Order this book online at www.trafford.com
or email orders@trafford.com

Most Trafford titles are also available at major online book retailers.

© Copyright 2012 Kelechikwu Emmanuel, Oguejiofor.

All rights reserved. No part of this publication may be reproduced, stored in a retrieval system, or transmitted, in any form or by any means, electronic, mechanical, photocopying, recording, or otherwise, without the written prior permission of the author.

Printed in the United States of America.

ISBN: 978-1-4669-6028-2 (sc)
ISBN: 978-1-4669-6029-9 (hc)
ISBN: 978-1-4669-6030-5 (e)

Library of Congress Control Number: 2012917957

Trafford rev. 09/24/2012

 www.trafford.com

North America & international
toll-free: 1 888 232 4444 (USA & Canada)
phone: 250 383 6864 ♦ fax: 812 355 4082

CONTENTS

ACKNOWLEDGMENTS ix

PREFACE xi

ABSTRACT xiii

CHAPTER 1: INTRODUCTION 1
   1.1 Background 1
   1.2 Introduction 3
   1.3 Problem Statements 6
   1.4 Research Objectives 7
   1.5 Research Questions 8
   1.6 Significance of the Study 9
   1.7 Scope of the Study 10
   1.8 Summary and Organization of Remaining Chapters 11

CHAPTER 2: LITERATURE REVIEW 13
   2.1 Introduction 13
   2.2 Organizational Commitment 14
       2.2.1 Organizational Characteristics 16
       2.2.2 Job Characteristics 16

2.2.3	Demographic Characteristics		17
2.2.4	Organizational Commitment Theory		18
2.2.5	Approaches to Organizational Commitment Theory		18
	2.2.5.1.	Sociological Commitment	19
	2.2.5.2.	Attitudinal Commitment	19
	2.2.5.3.	Moral Commitment	20
	2.2.5.4.	Behavioral Commitment	20
2.2.6	Core Theory of Organizational Commitment		22
	2.2.6.1.	Theory Content	22
	2.2.6.2.	The Antecedents of Organizational Commitment	23
	2.2.6.3.	The Consequences of Organizational Commitment	26
	2.2.6.4.	Organizational Commitment Questionnaire (OCQ)	28
	2.2.6.5.	Research Using the Organizational Commitment Questionnaire (OCQ)	29
2.3	Organizational Empowerment and Trust		31
2.3.1	Empowerment		31
	2.3.1.1	Kanter's Theory of Organizational Empowerment	33
	2.3.1.2	Components of Empowerment	34
2.3.2	Organizational Trust		36
2.4	Job Satisfaction		41
2.4.1	Education Level and Job Satisfaction		44
2.4.2	Age with Job Satisfaction		45
2.4.3	Gender with Job Satisfaction		46
2.5	Career Advancement Opportunity		48
2.6	Description of Variables and Conceptual Framework		51
2.6.1	Justification of variables		51
2.6.2	Independent Variables		51
2.6.3	Organizational Empowerment and Trust		52
2.6.4	Career Advancement Opportunities		52
2.6.5	Job satisfaction		53

  2.6.6 *Dependent variables* 54
  2.6.7 *Organizational commitment* 54
  2.6.8 *Moderating variables* 55
 2.7 Development of Hypotheses 56
 2.8 Summary 56

CHAPTER 3: METHODOLOGY 58

 3.1 Introduction 58
 3.2 Research Site, Population, and Sample 59
 3.3 Purpose of the Study and the Population 59
 3.4 Sample 60
  3.4.1 *Justification of the samples* 60
 3.5 Questionnaire 61
  3.5.1 *Dependent Variable (IV)* 61
  3.5.2 *Independent Variable (DV)* 61
 3.6 Data Collection Method 62
 3.7 Data Presentation and Analysis 63
 3.8 Conclusion 64

CHAPTER 4: FINDINGS 65

 4.1 Introduction 65
 4.2 Sample Characteristics 65
 4.3 Reliability Test 68
 4.4 Data Presentation 69
 4.5 Conclusions 77

CHAPTER 5: CONCLUSIONS 80

 5.1 Background 80
 5.2 Summary of Findings 80
 5.3 Recommendations 83

    5.3.1 Recruitment of Older Employees 83
    5.3.2 Enhancing Job Satisfaction 84
    5.3.3 Clear Career Advancement Opportunities 84
    5.3.4 Increasing Trust and Empowerment 85
5.4 Implications.. 85
5.5 Limitation of the Study.. 85
5.6 Suggestion for Future Research 86

REFERENCES 87

APPENDIX A 97

APPENDIX B 107

ACKNOWLEDGMENTS

To start with, I thank God, whom I know all glory and adoration is due. Who has given life and life begat all these accomplishments? I always know that I am not alone because factually that is not by my very own making that this journey was made, but from powers greater than me. Furthermore, from the bottom of my heart, I thank my parents whom to me represent God here on earth. Their relentless efforts and sacrifices have paid off with success to completing this work. And to whom else shall I owe this great honor in loyalty as I can't quantify that I deserve it at all but yet such an amazing privilege was given freely.

To top it all, I solemnly thank my research coordinator (Dr. Carlton) who has been a source of incredible momentum, which continuously propelled me at every point in completion of this work. Indeed it has been a privilege to share his knowledge and experience. I am also grateful to all research assistance and facilities from Derbyshire Business School, University of Derby. I am also much indebted for the priceless technical and moral support from the Raffles Education Group and all their partners as they inspired the standard of this work at length.

Finally, but not the least, I applaud all my friends and Mentors (Mr Pilayanthran and Dr. Leow Kah Loong). They did contribute immensely to the making of this success and also much love for Monica Pretty (Marketing Communication Manger at Hana International) who shared my inspiration during one of our brainstorming. I know there will be none like you all. All I can say is thank you all for such an investment. May peace, joy, and understanding be yours and sustain us all till the very end.

PREFACE

Mastering the Art of Sustainable Business Competitiveness is a master's thesis written in part fulfillment for the award of Master of Business Administration, University of Derby. This is a primary literature, which is a valuable contribution to business discipline. However, the main goal of publishing this classical piece of work is in line with my honorable desire to share the knowledge with the normal global citizens of the world whom might not necessarily have the paramount knowledge in the field of business discipline, giving them the opportunity to harness from this pool of knowledge. This work in essence would enable such individual to understand the relation of organizational commitment as the driving force to enhancing productivity and turnover.

This work is one of the single most comprehensive collections of postgraduate level creative work and research in the business world. My primary goal is to guide business leaders, managers, and even entrepreneurs on substantial matters of any organization's interest, which is maximizing share holders' capital or as said profit making; putting this in twenty-first-century context of intense competition, then the primary goal of any organization would be to **master the art of sustainable business competitiveness**, if they must thrive continuously in fulfilling their visions and mission statement.

And this is what makes this book much relevant than many. The findings of the research study shall be a guide for existing practitioners, especially to managers of multinational corporations or even entrepreneurs and human resource personnel's who share the mere desire of increasing the company's overall productivity and turnover. These findings shall guide them in mastering the art of sustainable business competitiveness. Finally, for any student who needs to study or pursue research in business-related field, such student shall also find this work as a master plan to guide him or her with practical composition to writing an excellent thesis.

ABSTRACT

This classical piece of work is in construct justification to propose a master plan to foster sustainable business competitiveness in any given organization. Notwithstanding that the empirical analysis was conducted on financial-related industries as it is porously linked to profit making which is somehow the bedrock of competitiveness of any organization. The main purpose of the research is to examine the relationship of organization commitment as the key ingredient in enhancing productivity and turnover of the given organization in any industry. The empirical analysis warranted the dispersal of 900 questionnaires to major economic cities in Malaysia (namely, the state of Johor, Penang, and Wilaya Presecutuan—Kuala Lumpur).

CHAPTER 1
Introduction

1.1 Background

In response to the theory and research suggesting that organizational empowerment and trust, career advancement opportunities, and job satisfaction impact several organizational outcomes, this study was designed to examine the relationship of organizational empowerment and trust, career advancement opportunities, and job satisfaction as a critical predictor of organizational commitment among bankers as well as the moderating effects of age, gender, and educational level on the outcome (organizational commitment).

Organizations perceived organizational commitment as one of the vital factor for the success of the organization. In order to run the organizations smoothly, effectively, and efficiently, the most valuable and indispensable factor organizations need is the human resource (Mosadeghrad 2003). Well-qualified and capable personnel are important in context of achieving goals and objectives of an organization. The success of an organization depends on the hardworking, loyal, and involved managers and employees. In this modern era where the world has become a global village, firms are considered to be competitive on the basis of competence of their human resources. It is somewhat a difficult task to handle people who are physically, psychologically, culturally, and ethnically different from each other. Accordingly, Luthans (2007) stated organizational commitment as "an attitude reflecting employees' loyalty to their organization and is an on-going process through which organizational participants express their concern for the organization and its continued success and well-being." Henkin and Marchiori (2003) defined organizational commitment as a feeling of employees which force them to be the part of their organization and recognize the goals, values, norms, and ethical standards of an organization. Shaw (2003) identified three dimensions of organizational commitment: affective, continuance. and normative commitment. Positive, sincere, and utmost involvement of employee for its organization is called affective commitment Continuance commitment can be seen when an individual is committed with the organization because of some specific benefits like pension, insurance, medical, and other fringe benefits. Employees' commitment with the organization because of the ethical standards or social norms is called normative commitment. According to Tella, Ayeni, and Popoola (2007) organizational commitment is the strongest motivator that highly affects persons' intentions to perform well, increases his efficiency, and improves his skills. Organizational commitment is important for organizations because it is a good predictor of organizational goals and objectives, productivity, absenteeism, and turnover.

However, not many organizations such as banks were paying much attention on this factor in order to enhance the commitment level of employees. Even though many of the banks realized the importance of organizational commitment, not many were aware which variables are the most important to focus on when their employees' commitment is low. Thus, various investigators have researched voluntary *employee* turnover intention within both the private and public *sectors* (Lu and Shiau 1997). However, little is known about the *employee* turnover intention or low in organizational commitment within the domestic private *banking* industry *in* Malaysia. Hence, one of the main objectives of this study is to integrate all the said predictor variables (organizational empowerment and trust, career advancement opportunities, job satisfaction) together with age, gender, and educational level impact on the criterion variable organizational commitment. The intended principal contribution of the current study to the organizational commitment literature is to ascertain the impact of predictor—criterion relationships on bankers in particular within the Malaysian context.

Thus, the present study is initiated in an attempt to bridge this gap in the study of organizational commitment by integrating the three bodies of literature of organizational empowerment and trust, career advancement opportunities, and job satisfaction together with age, gender, and educational level as moderators in the banking industry. Specifically, the present study examines both the direct and moderating effects on organizational commitment.

Benkhoff (1997) asserted that commitment is an exciting research issue because ignoring commitment is costly. Lack of commitment in "human service" professionals, that is, those who help others to improve the quality of their lives (Cherniss 1991), will lead to the loss of many skillful individuals from the organization whereby committed employees are characterized as loyal and productive members of the organization (Mowday, Porter, and Steers 1982; Steers 1977). As stated earlier, in today's highly competitive business environment, organizational survival and sustainable competitive advantage is dependent on committed employees (Woolridge 2000).

1.2 Introduction

Today, bank industry has become a very challenging industry in comparison to three decades ago due to the higher standard of living and purchasing power of consumers. The trend of this popularity could be seen clearly through their success after looking at the trend of how the Malaysian people did their banking style from a decade to another.

For instance, back to 1960s there were many employees who engaged their services in the banks, mainly front-line officer (teller) where most of the consumers have to be in the bank physically to do their banking transaction ranging from withdrawal, deposit, hire purchase, and other services. Then, automated teller machines (ATMs) were taking over in 1970s and 1980s. However, bigger changes were seen in 1990s and early 2000s, where those ATMs used to be the alternative avenue for banking purposes were taken over by Internet banking. The consumers could have better choice of performing their banking services from the banks. Nonetheless, these Internet banking services were not able to prolong their business' lives and were not as profitable as before when banks started to hit the Malaysian's consumers with mobile banking in mid-2000s.

According to Leonard (2000), besides providing the same services as in 1960s and 1970s, the banks now are not only providing basic services for consumers. There are some other services that are provided by the banks and those services include delivery of lost credit/debit cards, premium parking, ATMs, leading hotels and restaurants promotional rate, and even giving away 5-10% discount if their consumers are using their credit/debit cards during weekends or/and selected outlets. Alongside, icon hypermarkets and retailers like Carrefour, Tesco, Coffee Bean, and Baskin Robins tight up their business relationships with banks in order to generate more revenues to themselves and also to the banks.

This means that the banks are no longer the only place where the consumers do their basic banking services; they are also providing a wider range of services where it can be considered as a one-stop center for the consumers. In addition, the banks also provide additional services such as own in-house credit cards and mutual funds with an extensive line of products that provide an affordable alternative to the mainstream brands.

Bank industry had been doing well in Malaysia and some local banks have even set their footprints beyond Malaysia. Due to the nature of the business and their competitiveness in the market, almost all banks have made their present felt throughout Malaysia. For the purpose of this study, researcher would only focus on the banks in the state of Penang, Johor, and Wilayah Persekutuan, Kuala Lumpur, Malaysia. These banks had grown, set standards, and achieved enviable success at their very own way. They had been growing quite steadily and setting up branches from one state to another.

Due to the competitive pressures and increasing organizational complexity, most of these banks are facing with major problems such as employee turnover, low productivity, absenteeism, and low organizational commitment. One of the important factors that directly affected the problems is organizational commitment and therefore this study was carried out to determine what the factors were that drive to enhancing organizational commitment in order to reduce or eliminate the above mentioned problems.

Every discipline in the administrative sciences contributes in some way to helping organization to operate in a more effective and efficient way. High organizational commitment will increase organizational effectiveness and enable the organizations to achieve both its short-term and long-term goals in a more efficient way. It is also a central construct in sales, marketing, management, and psychology. As Balfour and Wechsler (1996) pointed out, overall organizational commitment is an appropriate question for those who are interested in organizational productivity and performance. While Sidle (2003) stated organizational commitment as dependent variable explaining multiple dimensions of organizational effectiveness such as adaptability, turnover, productivity, and tardiness rate. Becker (1960) posited that commitment is calculative. In contrast, Meyer and Allen (1991) and Mathieu, Bruvold, and Ritchey (2000) viewed commitment in terms of emotional attachment.

As we could see from the above explanation on the importance of organizational commitment, it is important for the bank industry to be aware that low organizational commitment will determine the success or the failure of their organizations. Therefore, this research was carried out in order to examine the impact of organizational commitment on bankers and nonbanker staff in bank industry.

As commitment is central to organizational life (Mowday 2000), and the degree of commitment is highly dependent on organizational empowerment and trust, career advancement opportunities, and job satisfaction, the present study is aimed to find out whether the integration of these three independent variables together with age, gender, and educational level (as moderators) will have the same results as earlier researches that were based on each variable acting independently on the criterion variable.

1.3 Problem Statements

The significance of turnover among bankers has been discussed in various studies (Dillard and Ferris 1979). For instance, Harrell (1990) found that high employee turnover in banking sector not only lead to the loss of valuable professionals (human capital) but also incur additional costs in recruitment and training of replacements as well as additional complications and uncertainties in planning operations. Besides that, the banking sector may also suffer degradation of their reputation and possible decline in clients' goodwill (Harrell 1990). Thus, it is the intent of this study to investigate the extent of the relationship between organizational empowerment and trust, career advancement opportunities, job satisfaction, and organizational commitment, and whether this relationship is moderated by age, gender, and educational level.

Extensive review of literature showed that organizational commitment is very weak across industries (Kimbell and Stonestreet 2000) and that the drastic drop in organizational commitment in the workforce is a direct result of the massive downsizing exercises carried out in the mid-1990s (Kimbell and Stonestreet 2000) that eroded the trust of the workforce in the unspoken personal contract of job security in exchange for loyalty and commitment to the organization that has been in force since the economic boom before World War II. Hence knowing how to cultivate organizational commitment in well-qualified employees is very important for sustainable organizational competitiveness contends. Mowday, Porter, and Steers (1982) emphasized that "highly committed employees are more desirous of remaining with the organization and working toward the organization's goals and hence be less likely to leave."

Thus, there is a dire need to examine the relationships of organizational empowerment and trust, career advancement opportunities, job satisfaction, and organizational commitment, and whether this relationship is moderated by age, gender, and educational level.

1.4 Research Objectives

The principal objective is to determine the relationship between organizational empowerment and trust, career advancement opportunities, and job satisfaction on organizational commitment. The research also aimed to understand the role of age, gender, and educational level as moderating variables because Cohen (1992) had imperatively called for future research on antecedents of organizational commitment to shift from main effect analysis to moderating effects. A meta-analysis performed by Mathieu and Zajac (1990) indicated a possible link between age, gender, and educational level on organizational commitment, and at the same time authors such as Van Vianen and Fisher (2002) also noted age, gender, and educational level differences in masculine/feminine culture preferred and suggested that the extent to which employees prefer masculine values is related to their hierarchical level. Specifically, the objective of this study is two-fold and is set out to:

(i) examine the relationship of organizational empowerment and trust, career advancement opportunities, and job satisfaction on organizational commitment;
(ii) investigate whether age, gender, and educational level moderate the above relationships.

Thus, this study endeavors to enhance the literature of organizational empowerment and trust, career advancement opportunities, job satisfaction, and organizational commitment together with age, gender, and educational level serve as moderators in the Malaysian context.

1.5 Research Questions

Given the above backdrop and in view of the above objectives, the questions that were addressed in this study are as follows:

a) Does organizational empowerment and trust directly predict organizational commitment of bankers?
b) Does a career advancement opportunity directly predict organizational commitment of bankers?

c) Does job satisfaction directly predict organizational commitment of bankers?
d) Do age, gender, and educational level significantly moderate the relationship of organizational empowerment and trust, career advancement opportunity, and job satisfaction in predicting organizational commitment of bankers?

1.6 Significance of the Study

The significance of the study can be seen from both theoretical and practical perspectives. From a theoretical perspective, this study provides an integration of three separate literatures, namely, organizational empowerment and trust, career advancement opportunities, and job satisfaction in examining their direct effects on organizational commitment as well as the moderating effect of age, gender, and educational level. From the practical perspective, the study expects to find the three independent variables, organizational empowerment and trust, career advancement opportunities, and job satisfaction, to be significant predictors of organizational commitment and the moderating effect of age, gender, and educational level, and will provide as a basic framework for practitioners who wish to adopt the model.

This study was conducted further to secure an understanding of the organizational commitment in bank industry. The study would be focusing on both the local and foreign banks throughout the states in Penang, Johor, and Wilayah Persekutuan, Kuala Lumpur, Malaysia. The study also intended to define organizational empowerment and trust, career advancement opportunities, job satisfaction, and organizational commitment.

Furthermore, with the in-depth understanding, the study helped to predict organizational commitment and to show how the independent variables play a significant role in the overall organizational commitment of the employees as well as how the moderating variables play their part in measuring organizational commitment level.

Besides that, it also could be a guide for the management to make decision related to organizational commitment. For example, the management is able to make wiser decision with the guidance of this study when there are any issues related to organizational commitment. Moreover, this research also allowed the management to view things from many angles and think creatively or able to walk out from "box' in decision making, especially with those issues related to organizational commitment.

This study also provides some recommendations to the organizations on how the organizational commitment of the employees can be enhanced. Moreover, it also provides assistance to the organizations in assessing organizational commitment. It also enables the organization to look at what are those variables to pay attention on when the employees' organizational commitment is not reaching the satisfactorily or expected level.

All in all, this research shall provide a better judgment in making wise and right decisions where the organizational commitment is very beneficial to the organization in both short run and long run in order to achieve its competitive advantage in order for the bank to remain relevant in this highly competitive industry.

1.7 Scope of the Study

This research attempts to examine the contributions of organizational empowerment and trust, career advancement opportunities, and job satisfaction on organizational commitment and to achieve set objectives;

data will be collected through questionnaires from respondents who are bankers employed by both local and foreign banks that are registered with the Institute of Bankers Malaysia (IBBM).

As this study is on the significance of organizational empowerment and trust, career advancement opportunities, and job satisfaction toward organizational commitment, the study's unit of analysis will be individuals (banker) whose answers to the questionnaires (Appendix A) will provide invaluable information to organizations on increasing organizational commitment.

1.8 Summary and Organization of Remaining Chapters

Chapter 1 introduces the background of the problem, explains the research problems, objectives to be achieved, research questions, and significance of the study. The remainder of this dissertation has been organized in the following manner:

Chapter 2 will focus on previous studies and their findings on organizational empowerment and trust, career advancement opportunities, and job satisfaction related to organizational commitment. This chapter will also present the theoretical framework and formulation of the research hypotheses based on filling the gap from previous studies.

Chapter 3 outlines the research methodology that is to be used in this study. The sample, measures used administration of the questionnaire, and data analysis techniques are all discussed in this chapter.

Chapter 4 gives a detailed profile of the respondents and descriptive analysis of the response. Discussion on the findings of the study is also presented in this chapter.

Chapter 5 recapitulates the findings and discusses the results generated from the study. This chapter concludes by discussing the theoretical and managerial implications, conclusion, and discussion on the limitations of the study. It will also include implications of the study and provide suggestions for future studies in this field.

CHAPTER 2
Literature Review

2.1 Introduction

In this chapter, we shall be reviewing the literature of organizational commitment from a few famous authors such as Porter (1976) and Mowday (1974) and others. Central to the present study is the idea that the more significant relationships of organizational empowerment and trust, career advancement opportunities, and job satisfaction, the more likely bankers are to be more committed to their organizations. This chapter would also provide the explanation of organizational characteristics, job characteristics, and demographic characteristics on organizational commitment.

Approaches to organizational commitment would also be explained, where the researcher would focus on the approaches such as sociological, attitudinal, moral, and behavioral commitment. These approaches would explain the differences of each commitment that are possessed by employees within the same organization. Core theory of organizational commitment would also be included.

Other than organizational commitment, organizational empowerment and trust would also be discussed in this chapter where the users would find the definition of each component and their importance. Kanter's theory of organizational empowerment and other researchers' work related to the organizational empowerment and trust were not neglected as well.

Besides that, this chapter would also review job satisfaction, where the literature review would be focusing on education level with job satisfaction, age with job satisfaction, and gender with job satisfaction. The users of this research paper would find the differences among those job satisfactions that are mentioned above. Career advancement opportunity would also be reviewed in the last section of the chapter and that to be followed with discussion on the theoretical framework and development of hypotheses for the present study.

2.2 Organizational Commitment

Colbert and Kwon (2000) mentioned that as organizations recognize the competitive advantage that can be gained through human resources, research on organizational commitment has gained its importance. Determining factors that are related to organizational commitment may be useful on several levels and its importance has increased dramatically when the right factors are determined. Mathieu and Zajac (1990) found organizational commitment to be strongly related to the intention to leave one's job and to the intention to search for job alternatives. They also found a positive relationship between organizational commitment and lateness as well as organizational commitment and turnover. Thus, a better understanding of the behavior and a better knowledge of the antecedents of organizational commitment will enable organizations to manage these withdrawal behaviors.

Porter et al. (1974) determined factors related to organizational commitment; it is vital to define the term as clear as possible in order to prevent confusion for the users of this study. They developed one commonly used definition of organization commitment. In their definition, three factors of organizational commitment were identified: a strong belief in and acceptance of the organization and a strong desire to remain in the organization. A fifteen-item organizational commitment questionnaire (OCQ) was developed to measure organizational commitment based on this definition. Besides Porter et al., Allen and Meyer (1990) did their studies and separated organizational commitment into three components: affective, continuance, and normative. The affective component refers to the employee's emotional attachment to, identification with, and involvement in the organization. The continuance component refers commitment based on the costs that the employee associates with leaving the organization. The normative component refers to the employees' feeling of obligation to remain with the organization. From their studies, Allen and Meyer (1990) developed a twenty-four-item scale to measure the three components of organizational commitment.

Whilst to that, Dunham, Grube, and Castaneda (1994) used confirmatory factor analysis to determine organizational commitment, as measured by the fifteen-item OCQ similar to affective commitment, normative commitment, or calculative commitment. Organizational commitment as measured by the OCQ converged with the affective component of organizational commitment and diverged from the normative and continuance components. The analysis showed that the OCQ measured affective commitment. Steers (1977) did the studies involving a variety of profession, including administrators, research scientist, and engineer; Curry et al. (1986) did the studies of employees in banking industry and police officers; while Dunham et al. (1994) have shown that a range of variables are related to organizational commitment. These variables include organizational characteristics, job characteristics, and demographic characteristics. A review of these variables allowed us to specifically consider those that may be related to the organizational commitment of employees with lower levels of authority, and in this study all the variables that make up the theoretical framework are derived from the above mentioned. It is hoped that with all the proven success from all the variables that have been worked out throughout the century, the variables that are used here will be able to predict the organizational commitment more accurately.

2.2.1 Organizational Characteristics

Employee's perceptions of organizational characteristics have been shown to be related to organizational commitment. One such characteristic, organizational empowerment and trust, was described by Colbert and Kwon (2000) as employee's perception of the extent to which the organization values their contribution and place more trust on the employees by letting them involve in making decision and to place a higher trust on them of getting their work done. Colbert and Kwon (2000) mentioned that organizational empowerment and trust was found to be positively related to the organizational commitment of hourly employees and managerial employees in factory. Other organization variables that have been found to be related to organizational commitment are instrumental communication found by Curry et al. (1986), group attitudes toward the organization by Steers (1977), and satisfaction with career advancement opportunities by Curry et al. (1986) and Quarles (1994).

2.2.2 Job Characteristics

Dimension of employee's jobs has also been related to organizational commitment. Dunham et al. (1994) used Hackman and Oldham's (1975) job diagnostic survey to measure the job characteristics of task identity, task significance, skill variety, autonomy, and feedback. All of these job characteristics were found to be positively related to organizational commitment. Steers (1977) examined the relationship between organizational commitment and four-core job dimension autonomy, variety, feedback, and task identity. When these variables were entered into a regression model as a group, they were found to be significantly related to organizational commitment; however, when entered separately, only task identity had a significant relationship to organizational commitment.

2.2.3 Demographic Characteristics

Additionally, several personal and demographic characteristics have been considered in studies of organizational commitment. Mathieu and Zajac (1990) found that age and organizational tenure are positively related to organizational commitment. Sommer, Bae, and Luthens (1996) also found that the increase of organizational commitment among Korean employees is related with age.

Gender is another personal characteristic that has been studied in relation to organizational commitment. Meta-analysis of Mathieu and Zajac (1990) found that women tend to be more committed than men, but the magnitude of the effect was small. However, Aven, Parker, and McEvoy (1993) used data from twenty-seven independent samples to examine the relationship between gender and attitudinal commitment. Their meta-analysis found that gender and attitudinal commitment were unrelated.

Level of education is another personal characteristic that has been related to organizational commitment. Steers (1977) found that the level of education was negatively related to organizational commitment. Mathieu and Zajac's (1990) meta-analysis confirmed this relationship and found that the relationship was significantly stronger for attitudinal commitment than for calculative commitment. They attribute this negative relationship to the greater number of job options that may be available to employees with higher levels of education.

From organizational characteristics to job characteristics and demographic characteristics, a lot of studies have been done and tried to relate them to organizational commitment. Some have been proven to be highly acceptable level, whereas some are not really relevant to all the characteristics that have been described. Therefore, the following literature will provide a better understanding for the users of this study about the factors that positively related to organizational commitment.

2.2.4 Organizational Commitment Theory

Organizational commitment is something very beneficial to organization and because of its importance there are several approaches to studying organizational commitment. Among those approaches that are vital for the success of the organization and through the literature review, four most significant approaches were found. The following paragraphs will be summarizing each approach from representative researches and definition of organizational commitment, followed by the core theory of organizational commitment theory proposed by Mowday, Steers, and Porter (1979). The related antecedents and consequences of organizational commitment would be shown. Meanwhile, OCQ and related research using OCQ would be included in this section as well.

2.2.5 Approaches to Organizational Commitment Theory

Li (2000) pointed out that organizational commitment can be viewed as having four significant approaches: (1) sociological commitment, (2) attitudinal commitment, (3) moral commitment, and (4) behavioral commitment.

2.2.5.1. Sociological Commitment

The first approach to examine the study of organizational commitment is sociological commitment by Kanter (1968). She defined commitment as the willingness of social actors to give their energy and loyalty to social systems, the attachment of personality systems to social relationship which is seen as self-expressive. She also identified three basic forms of commitment: continuance, control, and cohesion.

Continuance commitment is based on the idea that the cost of leaving an organization would be greater than the cost of staying. Control commitment is when the group members uphold the norms to obey the authority of the group. On the other hand, cohesion commitment is defined as an attachment to social relationship in an organization brought on by techniques such as public renunciation of previous social ties or by engaging in ceremonies that enhance group cohesion.

2.2.5.2. Attitudinal Commitment

The second approach to examine the study of organizational commitment is attitudinal commitment by Leonard (2000) and Mowday et al. (1982); Porter et al. (1974) defined it as when the goals of the organization and those of the individual become increasingly integrated or congruent. Leonard (2000) described this attitudinal commitment as the identification of the person to the organization. It is an attitude toward the organization that attaches the identity of the person to the organization.

Mowday et al. (1982) defined commitment as a partisan, affective attachment to the goals and values of an organization, to one's role in relation to goals and values, and to the organization for its own sake, apart from its purely instrumental worth. According to Porter et al. (1982), attitudinal commitment focuses on the process by which people come to think about their relationship with the organization. In many ways, it can be thought of as a mind set in which individuals consider the extent to which their own values and goals are congruent with those of the organization.

2.2.5.3. Moral Commitment

The third approach to examine the study of organizational commitment is moral commitment by Marsh and Mannari (1977) and Wiener and Gechman (1977). Concurrently, Tella et al. (2007) suggested that organizational commitment is moral involvement. He claimed it is a positive and high-intensity orientation based on internalization of organizational goals and values and identification with authority. Wiener and Gechman (1977) suggested that commitment behaviors are socially accepted behaviors that exceed formal and/or normative expectations relevant to the object of commitment. Marsh and Mannari (1977) stated that the committed employee considers it morally right to stay in the company, regardless of how much status enhancement or satisfaction the firm gives him or her over the year. Wiener and Gechman (1977) defined moral commitment as the aspect where the individual incorporates the values and goals of the organization into his/her own identity.

2.2.5.4. Behavioral Commitment

The fourth approach to examine the study of organizational commitment is behavioral commitment by Becker (1960); Kanter (1968); and Mowday et al. (1982). Becker (1960) suggested that commitment is viewed primarily as a function of individual behavior, and individuals become committed to the organization through their actions and choices over time. It is commitment-related behavior; the definition was formed based on the principle of consistent behavior and is also known as "calculated commitment." Hrebiniak and Alutto (1972) stated that it is defined as a structural phenomenon, which occurs as a result of individual—organizational transactions and alternations in side bets or investment over time.

Commitment comes into being when a person, by making a side bet, links extraneous with a consistent line of activity. Becker (1960) stated that side bets include unrelated aspects of the employees' life that retains organizational membership by the employee. However, Kirkman and Shapiro (2001) defined calculative commitment as the aspect of organizational commitment when the individual willingly remains with a particular system even when given an alternative job that provides slightly better outcomes for the individual.

According to Hrebiniak and Alutto (1972), behavioral commitment is an exchange relationship and investment aspect. It emphasizes that the individual has staked something of the value that indirectly relates to the current action and would be forfeited were he or she to deviate from certain consistent future behaviors. Individuals are bound by actions since there are side bets, sunk costs, and pension plans. They link themselves to the organization and cannot afford to separate themselves from the organization, according to Hrebiniak and Alutto (1972), and Mowday et al. (1982) described behavior commitment as related to the process by which individuals become locked into a certain organization and how they deal with this problem.

In summary, there are four categories for studying organizational commitment. According to Kanter (1968), sociological commitment includes continuance, cohesion, and control. On the other hand, Hrebiniak and Alutto (1972) mentioned that attitudinal commitment is an approach for studying organizational commitment, whereas Mowday et al. (1982) stated that moral involvement is another approach to organizational commitment. Finally, Becker (1960) mentioned that behavioral commitment is a function of individual behavior. After reviewing these four approaches to organizational commitment, it provides a deep understanding of various aspects of organizational commitment.

2.2.6 Core Theory of Organizational Commitment

Different researchers have applied different approaches to organizational commitment. In this study, the core theory of organizational commitment is based on Mowday et al. (1979) for the following reasons:

1. Various studies utilized the OCQ which is facilitated and developed by Mowday et al. (1979) and Steers and Porters (1979).
2. It covers largely attitudinal aspects and behavioral aspects of organizational commitment by Mowday et al. (1979).
3. It provides an operational and amenable empirical study of organizational commitment by Hrebiniak and Alutto (1972) and Mowday et al. (1979).

In this section, core theory of organizational commitment would be reviewed first and then followed by the antecedents and consequences of organizational commitment, the OCQ, and research using the OCQ.

2.2.6.1. Theory Content

Mowday et al. (1979) defined organizational commitment as a moral active and positive attitude toward the organization. It is the relative strength of an individual's identification with an involvement in a particular organization. There are three related factors for organizational commitment. Porter et al. (1974) and Cohen (1992) stated the factors as follows: (A) a willingness to exert considerable effort on behalf of the organization; (B) a strong belief in and acceptance of the organization's goals and values; and (C) a strong desire to maintain membership in the organization.

Mowday et al. (1982) suggested that the development of organizational commitment is a process that evolves through stages over time. There are antecedents and outcomes of organizational commitment. The antecedents include personal attributes, job characteristics, and work experiences. As part of this process, the four consequences of organizational commitment include job tardiness, job performance, job turnover, and job tenure. In the following paragraph, the antecedents of organizational commitment would be described first and then the consequences.

2.2.6.2. The Antecedents of Organizational Commitment

It has been suggested that organizational commitment is related to work experiences, personal attributes, and job and characteristics. Each of these antecedents would be described below:

(a) *Work experiences*

> According to Mowday et al. (1982), work experiences are viewed as a major socializing force and provide an important influence on organizational commitment. Still (1983) identified anticipatory socialization as one of the antecedent. Anticipatory, socialization plays an important role in the adjustment of an individual to an organization. Work experiences include organizational dependability, personal importance to the organization, leadership style, social involvement, and work relationship.
>
> There are positive relationships between organizational commitment and job satisfaction (Mowday et al. 1982), organizational dependability (Steers 1977), personal

importance to the organization (Steers 1977; Still 1983), directive leadership style (initiating structure) (Mathieu and Zajac 1990; Moon 2000), participative leadership style (Moon 2000; Mottaz 1986), leadership consideration (Moon 2000; Shaw et al. 2003), social involvement (Shaw et al. 2003; Still 1983), and work relationship (Moon 2000; Steers 1977).

When each of the above factors increases, the individual's organizational commitment increases as well. Table 2.1 depicts the antecedents from work experiences of organizational commitment.

Table 2.1: The Antecedents from Work Experiences of Organizational Commitment

The Antecedents of Organizational Commitment (+ indicates positive relationship; – indicates reverse relationship)	
Personal Attributes	**Relationship**
1. Organizational dependability	+
2. Job satisfaction	+
3. Personal importance	+
4. Directive leadership	+
5. Participative leadership	+
6. Social involvement	+
7. Work relationship	+

(b) *Personal attributes*

Besides work experiences, personal attribute also plays a significant role in affecting organizational commitment. Among those personal attributes that play their role include age, tenure, education, gender, perceived competence, and ability. These attributes were suggested by Hrebiniak and Alutto (1972); Marsh and Mannari (1977); Meyer and Allen (1984); and Still (1983).

Organizational commitment has been positively related to both age and tenure. Marsh and Mannari (1977) suggested that age should be more highly related to calculative commitment. When one's age or tenure increases, the individual's opportunities for alternative employment become more limited due the competition with younger employees as well as many other factors such as skills and age limit for certain task.

Meyer and Allen (1984) found that older workers become more attitudinally committed to the organization. However, education happened to have an inverse relationship to organizational commitment, according to Angle and Perry (1984); Mowday et al. (1982); Steers (1977); and Still (1983). While the studies by Angel et al. (1981); Gaines (1994); and Hrebiniak and Alutto (1972) suggested women are more committed than men. Gaines (1994) also stated that women are more committed than men, because they have more barriers to overcome than men. Gaines (1994) and Morrow (1983) also found a positive relationship between organizational commitment and perceived competence and ability. Table 2.2 depicts the antecedents from personal attributes of organizational commitment.

Table 2.2: The Antecedents from Personal Attributes of Organizational Commitment

The Antecedents of Organizational Commitment (+ indicates positive relationship; – indicates reverse relationship)	
Personal Attributes	**Relationship**
1. Age	+
2. Tenure	+
3. Education	–
4. Gender	Female +
5. Perceived competence	+
6. Ability	+

(c) Job characteristics

Other than work experiences and personal attribute, job characteristics also acting as antecedents to organizational commitment include job scope and role overload. These were suggested by Marsh and Mannari (1977); Mowday et al. (1982); and Steers (1977); as job scope increases the individual's challenge, organizational commitment increases. However, role overload was strongly and inversely related to organizational commitment, according to Marsh and Mannari (1977) and Mowday et al. (1982). The job should be clear and challenging for positive influence. Once it becomes ambiguous and stresses increase, the effect would be adverse. Behrman and Perreault (1984) and Marsh and Mannari (1977) mentioned that once there are greater levels of role stress, this leads to lower organizational commitment. Table 2.3 depicts the antecedents from job characteristics of organizational commitment.

Table 2.3: The Antecedents from Job Characteristics of Organizational Commitment

The Antecedents of Organizational Commitment (+ indicates positive relationship; – indicates reverse relationship)	
Job Characteristics	**Relationship**
1. Job scope	+
2. Role overload	–
3. Role stress	–

2.2.6.3. *The Consequences of Organizational Commitment*

Organizational commitment is linked to job tardiness, job tenure, job performance, and job turnover. A discussion of each of these consequences of organizational commitment is presented as follows:

(a) *Job tardiness*

Angel et al. (1981); Mathieu and Zajac (1990); and Mowday et al. (1982) stated that there is a strong and inversely significant correlation between job tardiness and organizational commitment. The greater the organizational commitment of the individual, the less job tardiness will be.

(b) *Job tenure*

Mathieu and Zajac (1990) and Mowday et al. (1982) mentioned that there is a highly significant positive correlation between increased job tenure and increased organizational commitment. The longer the job tenure of individuals, the greater the organizational commitment will be.

(c) *Job performance*

Mathieu and Zajac (1990); Mowday et al., (1974); Porter et al., (1976); and Steers (1977) stated that relationship between organizational commitment and job performance is not strong. Yet, even when it is weak, there is still a statistically significant positive correlation between job performance and organizational commitment. Mowday et al. (1982) mentioned that commitment may influence the amount of effort an employee puts forth on the job and this effort should influence actual performance.

(d) *Job turnover*

Angle and Perry (1981); Mathieu and Zajac (1990); Mowday et al. (1982); Porter et al. (1976); and Steers (1977) stated that there is high and inverse significant correlation between job turnover and organizational commitment. The more the organizational commitment of the individual, the less job turnover will be. Figure 2.1 graphically summarizes the combination of relationships of the antecedents and consequences of organizational commitment.

Figure 2.1: The Antecedents and Consequences of Organizational Commitment Model
(+ indicates positive relationship; − indicates reverse relationship)

Antecedents		Consequences
	Personal Attributes	
1. Age +		Job performance +
2. Tenure +		
3. Education −		
4. Gender (female +)		
5. Perceived competence +		
6. Ability +		Job tenure +
	Job Characteristics	
1. Job scope +		Job tardiness −
2. Role overload −		
3. Role stress −		
	Work Experiences	
1. Organizational dependability		Job turnover −
2. Job satisfaction +		
3. Personal importance +		
4. Directive leadership +		
5. Participative leadership +		
6. Social involvement +		
7. Work relationship +		

2.2.6.4. Organizational Commitment Questionnaire (OCQ)

Hrebiniak and Alutto (1972) stated that there is a lack of extensive examination of the organizational commitment of professionals which might be due to the difficulty of making that concept operational and of deriving indexes amendable to empirical testing and validation.

From there in 1979, Mowday et al. developed an OCQ instrument with the intention to overcome the above shortcoming. They defined organizational commitment as the relative strength of an individual's identification with an involvement in a particular organization. This is also been supported by Painter (1994) and Porter et al. (1974). The OCQ instrument was designed to measure the degree to which subjects feel committed to the employing organization; 2,563 employees were chosen as their sample in nine organizations for measuring the attitudinal aspects over a time span of nine years.

The OCQ instrument contains fifteen statements; the OCQ have the items pertaining to the subject's perceptions concerning the loyalty toward the organization, the willingness to exert a great deal of effort to achieve organizational goals, and the acceptance of the organization's values. All statements represent statements to which the subject responds on seven-point Liker-type scales, ranging from "strongly disagree" to "strongly agree." The wording of six statements is reversed in an attempt to reduce response set bias, according to Mowday et al. (1979).

2.2.6.5. Research Using the Organizational Commitment Questionnaire (OCQ)

More than two studies applied the OCQ with further investigation with other variables and validation of the model. Angle and Perry (1983) applied the OCQ with side bets and employee satisfaction to test the factors leading to organizational commitment. They found that the extrinsic aspects of satisfaction were more strongly associated with organizational commitment than were intrinsic aspects. Deakin and Boussouara (2000) used the OCQ instrument to study 764 male professional accountants and their organizational commitment at different career stages. They found the older the respondent was the higher the organizational commitment.

Gaines (1994) applied the OCQ in their research and utilized organizational commitment as a connector between job satisfaction and intent to leave for retail turnover process investigation research. Gupta and Jenkins (1992) applied the OCQ to investigate the influence of organizational formalization upon work alienation and organizational commitment. They found that formalization influenced organizational commitment indirectly by its effects on role ambiguity and role conflict.

Harrel (1990) applied OCQ in cross-cultural setting. The study tested Japanese employees in Japan, and a fair degree of validity resulted in Japanese organizations. Podsakoff, MacKenzie, and Bommer (1995) utilized the OCQ scale to assess an employee's identification with an involvement in an organization. They found the OCQ possesses adequate psychometric properties, and the data pertaining to its reliability and validity are generally positive. Sloan (1999) and Cook and Wall (1980) used OCQ communication banks questionnaire to test the relationship between organizational commitment and organizational communication satisfaction in three Guatemalan organizations. Their results confirmed the validity of the OCQ in Guatemala as a result from the study of Mowday et al. (1979). Thus, the OCQ is a reliable model for testing the organizational commitment factor, supported by Angle and Perry (1986); Podsakoff, MacKenzie, and Bommer (1995); and Sloan (1999). The OCQ will also be used in order to measure the organizational commitment in this study.

2.3 Organizational Empowerment and Trust

2.3.1 Empowerment

Employee empowerment is loosely defined as giving employees the freedom to do whatever is necessary to create customer satisfaction. Empowerment has been credited as a primary factor in the phenomenal success of businesses in Japan and other countries in Europe, according to Benson (1991); Byham (1992); and Navran (1992). Research shows that those organizations that empower their employees experience increased morale and productivity. While there is recognition that empowerment will enable businesses to thrive in the fiercely competitive marketplace of the future, mentioned by Byham (1992) and Navran (1992).

Bowen and Lawler (1992) defined empowerment as giving employees:

a) power to make decisions,
b) rewards based on how well the organization performs, and
c) information about organizational performance and how to contribute to the organization.

Byham (1992) added that recognition of and respect for the employee adds to the feeling of empowerment. To fully utilize human capital, i.e., employees, Stanley (2001) advised managers to find ways to trust their workers in making decisions. Byham (1992) noted that leaders in empowering organizations are characterized by openness and receptivity to new ideas as well as by their caring and respectful attitude. He added that encouraging innovation in how employees do their jobs and opening access to information that helps employees understand how to improve their performance creates the environment of empowerment. Barriers to empowerment include the following: a lack of managerial commitment to the concept; an unwillingness to change on the part of the employee and/or employer; a reluctance on the part of employees to take on the responsibility of making decisions; poor communication between employees and employers; and the failure to realize that in the short run, performance may dip as empowerment is implemented.

Since empowerment is linked to productivity and business success. As a means of improving productivity, customer service, and organizations are taking the approach that the person who first deal problem should have the power to solve it. Several investigators stress importance of participative decision making and empowerment, with increase employee self-efficacy (Conger and Kanugo 1988), job satisfaction (Spector 1986), and task motivation (Thomas and Velthouse 1990). Empowerment occurs when employees are given the opportunity to control their work environment and influence decisions that affect them and their organization. Besides the definition and the importance of empowerment that we have seen above, following paragraphs will be looking at the empowerment studies that are carried out by other scholars in order to give the clearer picture for the users of this research paper.

Thomas and Velthouse (1990) cited Zimmerman's definition of empowerment: "a multi-level construct that occurs at three levels: individual, in relation to psychological and behavioral variables; organizational, in relation to resource mobilization and participatory opportunities; and community, relating to socio-political structure and social change." Zimmerman (1995) mentioned that the construct of psychological empowerment at the individual level includes beliefs that goals can be achieved, awareness about resources and factors that hinder or enhance one's efforts to achieve those goals, and efforts to fulfill the goals.

Seen as a motivational construct, organizational empowerment can be defined as a process of enhancing feelings of self-efficacy among organizational members through the identification of conditions that foster powerlessness and through their removal by both formal organizational practices and informal techniques of providing efficacy information by Conger and Kanungo (1988).

Zimmerman (1995) defined a more global definition of empowerment as it is an intentional ongoing process centered in the local community, involving mutual respect, critical reflection, caring, and group participation, through which people lacking an equal share of valued resources gain greater access to and control over those resources.

2.3.1.1 Kanter's Theory of Organizational Empowerment

Kanter (1977) argued that people react rationally to the situations in which they find themselves. When situations are structured in such a way that employees feel empowered, the organization is likely to benefit both in terms of the attitudes of employees and the organization's effectiveness. In fact, she argued that the impact of organizational structures on organizational behavior is far greater than the impact of employee personality predisposition.

The organizational structures that Kanter (1977) believed particularly important to the growth of empowerment are as follows: having access to information, receiving support, having access to resources necessary to do the job, and having the opportunity to learn and grow. Access to these empowering structures is facilitated by formal job characteristics. That is, jobs that are visible and central to the organization's goals and that allow the employee flexibility enhance empowerment. In addition, informal job characteristics such as alliances with superiors, peers, and subordinates within the organization further influence empowerment. According to Kanter's theory, the mandate of management is to create conditions for work effectiveness by ensuring employees have access to the information, support, and resources necessary to accomplish work as well as are provided ongoing opportunities for employee development. Having access to these structures will result in increased levels of organizational commitment, feelings of autonomy, and self-efficacy. Consequently, employees are more productive and effective in meeting organizational goals.

2.3.1.2 Components of Empowerment

In illustrating empowerment, Zimmerman (1995) described the interrelationships of empowerment as involving three distinct components—interpersonal, interactional, and behavioral.

The interpersonal component pertains to people's self-perceptions and their beliefs about their ability to influence their environment and significant others. It includes perceived control, competence, motivation control, and self-efficacy. It is unlikely that individuals who do not believe that they have the capability to achieve goals would either learn about what it takes to achieve those goals or do what it takes to accomplish them, according to Zimmerman (1995).

The interactional component relates to the degree to which individuals understand their community and related sociopolitical issues. Zimmerman (1995) noted that this aspect of psychological empowerment suggests that people are aware of behavioral options or choices to act as they believe appropriate to achieve goals they set for themselves. Included in this component is decision making, problem solving, and leadership skills.

The behavioral component refers to the actions people take that have a direct influence on outcomes. Examples of empowerment behaviors include directing a work team or becoming involved in spearheading the organization's charity drive. This component also includes behaviors to manage stress and adapt to change.

Conger and Kanungo (1988) proposed that empowerment be viewed in two ways—as a relational construct and as a motivational construct. As a relational construct, empowerment describes the perceived power or control that an individual has over others and refers to the act of delegating authority. Considered in this manner, empowerment can be interpreted as the process by which a leader shares power with subordinates. Because this is such a common practice, employee participation and employee empowerment are often considered to be the same. However, they believed that this perspective does not sufficiently address how subordinate employees experience empowerment; they raised some questions that impact how empowerment is driven:

"For example, does sharing of authority and resources with subordinates automatically empower them? Through what psychological mechanisms do participative and resource-sharing techniques foster an empowering experience among subordinates? Are participation and the sharing of organizational resources the only techniques for empowerment? Are the effects of an empowering experience the same as the effects of delegation, participation, and resource sharing?"

As a motivational construct, empowerment refers to an intrinsic need for self-determination or a strong belief in self-efficacy. Consequently, Conger and Kanungo (1988) theorized that power is based in one's motivational disposition: "Any managerial strategy or technique that strengthens this self-determination need or self-efficacy belief of employees will make them feel more powerful. Conversely, any strategy that weakens the self-determination need or self-efficacy belief of employees will increase their feelings of powerlessness." They also noted that empowerment as an enabling process affects both initiation and persistence of subordinates' task behavior. That is, when employees are enables, they are more likely to initiate tasks and persist to completion; they feel empowered. To clarify this concept, Conger and Kanungo (1988) stated as follows:

"The strength of peoples' conviction in their own effectiveness is likely to affect whether they would even try to cope with given situations.... They get involved in activities and behave assuredly when they judge themselves capable of handling situations that would otherwise be intimidating . . . . Efficacy expectations determine how much effort people will expand and how long they will persist in the face of obstacles and aversive experiences."

These questions point out that it takes more than just setting up the parameters of organizational empowerment to achieve results; specific activities on the part of the leadership are vital to supplement the organization's program.

2.3.2 Organizational Trust

Organizational trust is particularly appropriate when an external consultant is asked to intervene in an organization. For instance, the bankers of the firm must have trust in both the ability and the intentions of the consultant. Boussouara and Deakins (2000) noted that trust competence is highly influenced by organization member's view of the consultant's capacity to understand their organization and to take into account its unique attributes and concerns.

As an outcome, trust refers to the relationship, which organization members have. When people embedded in a social system together examine values and norms that shape behavior in that system, and envision new values, the result can be increased understanding and trust. Heather et al. (2001) argued that the most important roles of trust concern issues on how and why organizational knowledge may develop.

As current organizations restructure and reengineer in the name of efficiency and effectiveness, trust in management has become an increasingly important element in determining organizational climate, employee performance, and commitment to the organization. Employees who have survived downsizing are understandably wary about the future direction of the organization and their roles within it. Curry et al. (1986) defined organizational trust as the extent to which one is willing to ascribe good intentions to and have confidence in the words and actions of other people. Heather et al. (2001) stated that trust has a significant impact on important organizational factors such as group cohesion, perceived fairness of decisions, organizational citizenship behavior, job satisfaction, and organizational effectiveness mistrust results when information is withheld, when resources are allocated inconsistently, and when employees have no support from management.

From the definition above, we can see the importance of the organizational trust. Without this organizational trust, people are difficult to work together except under conditions of stringent control. Ironically, at a time when trust is most needed for successful organizational transformation, the changes resulting from restructuring have diminished trust within the work setting. This state of affairs has serious implications for organizational performance. According to Heather et al. (2001), nurses, the largest group of health-care providers in hospitals, have been particularly hard hit by recent downsizing. It is quite possible that their mistrust of the system could potentially threaten the quality of patient care.

Meanwhile, Kanter (1977) defined organizational trust as to maintain work environments that provide access to information, resources, support, and the opportunity to learn and develop which are empowering and enable employees to accomplish their work. As a result, employees are more satisfied with their work and sense that management can be trusted to do whatever is necessary to ensure that high-quality outcomes are achievable. According to her, the employees in environments such as these are more committed to the organization and more likely to engage in positive organizational activities.

Therefore, trust is increasingly important to organizational relationships, particularly in light of dramatic organizational changes designed to flatten organizational structures and place more decisional control in the hands of front-line employees. According to Kanter (1977), trust evolves from a mutual understanding based on shared values and is essential from employee loyalty and commitment.

Gilbert and Tang (1998) defined organizational trust as the belief that an employer will be straightforward and follow through on commitments. Trust refers to employee faith in organizational leaders and the belief that ultimately organizational actions will prove beneficial for employees. Mishra and Spreitzer (1988) stated that open communication, sharing of critical information, sharing of perceptions and conditions of trust: discreteness, availability, competence, consistency, fairness, integrity, loyalty, openness, overall trust, promise fulfillment, and receptivity.

Trust must be an integral and coherent part of the organizational culture if change is to be implemented effectively and sustained. According to Mishra and Spreitzer (1988), empowering employees involves understanding the needs and capabilities of the employees, trusting them, and helping them to maximize their fulfillment while pursuing corporate goals. Mutual trust is a critical component of this process. Managers must be willing to empower employees and employees must accept the challenge inherent in empowerment and commit to organizational goals. According to Heather et al. (2001), high levels of organizational trust are needed to accomplish change, yet paradoxically, the change itself may destroy trust and threaten organizational effectiveness. Research on organizational downsizing has shown that decreased levels of trust are associated with decreased communication and increased conflict. As continue to downsize, employee trust and morale are eroded as workloads increase and job insecurity escalates. In such low trust organizations, behaviors such as high absenteeism, prolonged breaks, limited learning, low accountability, reactionary thinking, and low creativity are predictably common (Heather et al. 2001).

While Kramer, Brewer, and Hanna (1993) stated that in order to maintain that employees in low power/low status positions depend on others for a variety of critical organizational resources and that uncertainty limits access to information needed to make judgments about trustworthiness. Similarly, Heather et al. (1991) claims that vulnerability and uncertainty are central to the issue of trust and those violations of trust take on greater significance for those in relatively low power/control positions, such as hospital staff nurses.

According to Kramer et al. (1993), managers play a crucial role in the development of trust since they control the flow of information by sharing or not sharing key information. The degree of trust within an organization depends on managerial philosophy, organizational actions and structures, and employees' expectations of reciprocity. Gilbert and Tang (1998) also found a strong positive relationship between organizational trust and the nature and extent of organizational communication. They suggested that formal, but even more importantly informal, access to organizational communication channels enhances organizational trust. The impact of trust on organizational outcomes has been reported in the organizational literature.

Podsakoff, Mackenzie, and Bommer (1996) found organizational trust to be significantly related to job satisfaction, organizational commitment, role clarity, and in-role performance. Kramer et al. (1993) linked employee empowerment in a large manufacturing firm to an atmosphere of mutual trust. Mishra and Spreitzer (1998) found that 90% of managers surveyed in their study felt that trust starts at the top an organization and trickles down. Organizational effectiveness was perceived to depend on the level of organizational trust. Trust was associated with effective decision making as a result of sharing ideas, information, and feelings, organizational credibility, and increased productivity. Organizational ineffectiveness was attributed to employee distrust of management by 79.4% of those surveyed. Mishra and Spreitzer (1998) concluded that organizational empowerment and trust have a significant impact on job design, control mechanisms, extent and effectiveness of communication, relationships with other units, and degree of innovation, job satisfaction, commitment, organizational citizenship behaviors, goal sharing, and crisis management.

There is little empirical research in the nursing literature and many other industries relating to organizational trust. Couple of the survey includes survey of staff nurses in a small United States hospital; Kramer and Schmalenberg (1993) concluded that trust was the best predictor of feelings of autonomy and empowerment.

In another nursing study, McDaniel and Sutmpf (1993) found that nurses were more empowered in health-care organizations where information is shared and trust levels are high. Li (2000) emphasized the importance of leadership behavior in developing and maintaining trust levels in nursing work settings. Thus, we can see the importance of the organizational trust as distrust among employees as well as among management will affect the effectiveness of the organization in today's turbulent work environments.

There are several approaches used by different researchers to measure the empowerment in many industries. One of the way is through empowerment structures described by Kanter (1977); access to opportunity, information, support, and resources, it has been used to measure nurses' perception from all areas of Ontario by Enriquez et al. (2001). While the twelve-item instruments of interpersonal trust at work scale (ORS) are further used by Enrique et al. (2001) to measure nurses trust and confidence of their management and peers level in the organization. Both measures show the reliability coefficient between 70 and 85.2. However, for this research purpose a similar type of questionnaire will be used in this study in order to measure organizational empowerment and trust for the executive and nonexecutive level in the bank industry.

2.4 Job Satisfaction

Job satisfaction involves the satisfaction that is being derived from engaging in work. It is an attitude or an end feeling that the employees experience after completing a task. From the literature review, employees who are happy with their job contribute in a more positive way toward organization. Locke (1969) defined job satisfaction as the pleasurable emotional state resulting from the appraisal of one's job as achieving or facilitating the achievement of one's job values.

According to Krishnaswamy (1993), job satisfaction can be derived through individuals themselves. Individuals must first determine their needs and wants and then rank them in terms of importance. Specific activities to be achieved such as setting own goal in achieving the needs and wants and prioritizing the tasks necessary to accomplish them, these activities seem to be easy to state down; however, not many employees failed to task is more important than the other.

An extensive review of the literature by Forsyth (1995) indicated the more important factors conductive to job satisfaction, that is, the work-related variables:

1) Mentally challenging work
2) Equitable rewards
3) Supportive working conditions/environment
4) Supportive colleagues

Johns (1996) stated that job satisfaction from the work itself often results when the employee can control the pace and method of operating on the job, can utilize skills and abilities in a variety of ways, and can complete identifiable whole jobs.

Studies by Yoong (1997) have shown that organizational commitment procedures falls under the category of equitable rewards as well as the supportive working conditions/environment. From an executive's viewpoint and perspective, high organizational commitment helps in the creation of a supportive working environment. This is also conductive for one's own personal career growth. Macan (1994) stated that it was expected that those who felt in the supportive working condition would be most satisfied with their job.

Yoong (1997) also asserted that employees with higher organizational commitment tend to have less stress for the employees, which means the employees will be more efficient, satisfied, healthy employees, which in turn means more effective organizations. Satisfaction on the job carries over the employees' off-the-job hours. One can therefore deduce and conclude that the goal of high job satisfaction for the employees can be defended in terms of both dollars and cents and social responsibility, according to Yoong (1997).

Stanley (2001) mentioned that employees with high levels of job satisfaction are positive about their workplace. Every manager should work diligently to increase job satisfaction, because high job satisfaction leads to high productivity, low absenteeism, low turnover, and low rates of major setbacks like heart disease and stroke. In addition, employees who are happy with their jobs contribute in a more positive way toward society; however, low job satisfaction can turn an exciting career into a dreaded workplace.

Maccoby (1988) stated that if self-developers are struck in dead end of dissatisfying jobs, they will look for a better work and meanwhile, find new ways to express themselves inside or outside the company. Johns (1996) stated that a determinant of job dissatisfaction is perceived communication inequity. Judgment of equity and inequity in perceived communication affect the individuals' perceptions of job satisfaction/dissatisfaction.

Yoong (1997) stated that the final point to note is the support of job satisfaction's importance is the spin-off effect that job satisfaction has for society as a whole as some benefits of job satisfaction accrue to every citizen in society. Satisfied employees are more likely to be satisfied citizens. Yoong (1997) also mentioned that these people would then hold a more positive attitude toward life in general and make for a society of more psychologically healthy people.

Robbins (1996) indicated that managers should therefore persistently do everything they can to enhance the job satisfaction of each and every employee concerned. The importance of job satisfaction is clear. Managers should therefore be concerned with the level of job satisfaction in their organization because:

1) There is a clear evidence that dissatisfaction employees are more likely to resign.
2) It has been demonstrated that satisfied employees have better health and live longer.
3) Satisfaction on the job carries over to the employees' life outside the job.

Yoong (1997) mentioned that there are many popular literatures on organizational commitment resulting in increased job performance and satisfaction and fewer job tensions; surprisingly, a theoretical framework and empirical examinations are lacking. Perhaps it is because organizational commitment is typically viewed as a fad and not held in very high esteem by researchers in the field. Nonetheless, he also stated that many organizations are trying to increase the employees' commitment toward the organization by promoting the awareness of the importance of good career advancement opportunities, organizational trust as well as training and development courses.

2.4.1 Education Level and Job Satisfaction

There are some studies by Vollmer and Kinney (1955); Wiener and Gechman (1977); and Yoong (1997) which show that the effects of education on the job satisfaction could be negative. In this situation, employees who had received formal education may be dissatisfied with the routine tasks that have to be performed in the organization as required for most of the jobs. Correlation of the increased in education level and the job satisfaction will be negative also shown in other studies, mentioned by Johns (1996).

Saiyaddin (1985) had studied on the relationship between job satisfaction and personal characteristics on a sample of 778 Indians and 620 Nigerians. In that study, it shows that the job satisfaction decreases when the level of education rises for both the Indians and Nigerians. Higher expectations are expected for the higher level of education and if the works that the employees perform do not fulfill this expectation, then dissatisfaction among the workers is experienced. It shows that highly educated employees are dissatisfied doing routine jobs in their working area.

2.4.2 Age with Job Satisfaction

Many studies have sought to explain age variation in job satisfaction. Mottaz (1986) listed four possible explanations to account these variations. Young workers usually look at their jobs differently than older workers. In the study of Stanley (2001), it was found that job satisfaction concerns associated with young workers focus on desire for recognition, quick promotions, and good pay. When they do a splendid job they must be rewarded promptly. They need the reinforcement. Plenty of time is also important. Most young people have grown up accustomed to having time to pursue a variety of leisure activities. They require time away from work to recharge. Young workers are a dynamic force for change. Today's young workers are tomorrow's leaders. They should be acknowledged for their creativity and unlimited ideas for improvement.

In the same study, Stanley (2001) found that older workers have different ideas about job satisfaction. Job security is one of the most important job satisfaction components for older workers. Steady promotional advancement and scheduled pay increases provide consistency for this group. Older workers want their job responsibilities defined. They will commit themselves to the task at hand and are willing to work overtime to finish a project. Older workers value their elevated status in the group as significant. They are mature in their thinking and feel seniority and past accomplishments should be valued. Their allegiance to the organization is relatively strong.

Stanley (2001) also stated that older workers have a traditional view of organizational life, and job satisfaction is tied to this perspective. They grew up in time when hierarchical systems were utilized to maintain structure within organizations. It was an orderly method for an orderly time.

Today, the global economy has created rapid change. The traditional view may still be worthwhile, but organizations must be able to respond to market forces more swiftly now. This change requires new ideas and ways interacting that differ from the traditional view of organizational life. Nevertheless, young workers who are high achievers need to be recognized and rewarded. This may impact the job satisfaction of old workers; older workers can be further motivated through proper recognition and job assignments. For the most part, older workers have established successful organizational structure in the past and can adapt to future changes.

2.4.3 Gender with Job Satisfaction

Previous research indicated that there were some inconsistencies in the job satisfaction related to the gender differences. Some studies such as the studies by Quarles (1994) and Robbins (1996) had found women to be more satisfied than men, whereas other studies like the studies by Johns (1996) showed men to be more satisfied than women. What we can draw from here is the different level of job satisfaction for men and women; women have different expectation with regards to work, which is supported by Porter et al. (1974).

To men, it was revealed that careers were central importance but not as important to women, according to Porter et al. (1974). This shows that job satisfaction is seen as emotional response resulting through the interaction of work rewards and work values. The greater the perceived congruence between rewards and value, the greater the job satisfaction. Shaw et al. (2003) suggested that women placed more value on the social factors of a job than men and they valued the opportunity for self-expression in their work rather than women. Johns (1996) found that females like to work in the pleasant employees rather than male. However, men are more regarded to influence important decision and direct the work of others as more important. Therefore, job satisfaction is seen as a function of what is expected and what is received.

The argument here is although women receive less from their jobs than men, they have lower expectation and hence perceived themselves as being just as satisfied as men. Murray and Atkinson (1981) further investigated these arguments and the reasoned that if the expectancy notion was correct, then women should be more satisfied than men if job level and work rewards are held constant. However, other studies show that men and women do not indicate differences in overall job satisfaction, as cited by Quinn, Staines, and McCullough (1974).

In other findings, it is indicated that women generally have lower status jobs, are paid much less, and have fewer opportunities for promotion and other rewards compared with men. In this situation, the only explanation given based on expectancy explanation was that men and women have different expectation with regard to work, as stated by Quinn et al. (1974) and Sidle (2003). Although women received less from their jobs than men, they have lower expectation and hence perceive themselves as being just as satisfied as men. Based on the value explanation, on the similar level of work satisfaction reported for the two sexes is that men and women may use qualitatively different criteria in their assessment of work. While Johns (1996) had studied data from 1,385 workers representing a variety of occupation and indicated that there is no significant differences between men and women in overall work satisfaction within either upper level or lower level occupational categories. His results do not support the expectancy explanation but provide conditional support for the value explanation.

2.5 Career Advancement Opportunity

Painter (1994) conducted a study of job satisfaction and the results showed that the extrinsic rewards of salary, career advancement, and organizational trust were the most significant predictors of overall job satisfaction.

Gaines (1994) wrote an article on career advancement and job satisfaction. He found that one approach to keep employees dedicated and productive when traditional rewards cannot be given is to help employees take charge of their career advancement or development and job satisfaction. This can be done by helping employees assess their skills, determining what they like and dislike about their job and identify areas they would like to develop or change. This type of process encourages people to probe deeply into motivating them and what would make their work more satisfying. Organizations then prepare employees to negotiate what their managers redesign their jobs to make better use of their strengths and serve their personal goals as well as the organization's goals.

Forsyth (1995) mentioned that at the Steel Service Institute's 1994 annual convention, Roger Herman, author of "Keeping Good People," told his audience that improving the work environment and placing more value on employee's career advancement strengthens job satisfaction and company loyalty.

Kramer et al. (1993) found that with the splintering of traditional career ladders, employers can no longer manage their workers' careers, but instead must encourage and teach them career advancement or career self-management. He discussed the various components of a satisfying career as well as the benefits of lateral moves. To encourage talent that cannot advance, progressive corporations are working to develop career coaches, who give staff members the truth about what is happening in the organization and prepare them for the inevitable changes in the employment contract. Companies are also encouraging employees to use internal job-posting systems to search for potential lateral assignments as a way of keeping their interest in the company. Finally, compensation systems are being redesigned to support career advancement or career management initiatives in a variety of ways, including skill-based pay, variable pay, and broad banding.

In the case studies of career development planning and job satisfaction, Painter (1994) indicated that through a variety of programs, the Employee Development Centre, a resource for career guidance within Texas Instruments Incorporation's Systems and Services Division, helps information systems and services (IS&S) employees better understand what they want from their careers and how to achieve their goals. Since its opening in April 1991, the center has seen more than 2,000 employees. The center's goals are based on three conclusions:

1) Structured training improves job skills, thereby increasing job effectiveness.
2) An environment that encourages individual initiative for self-development supports IS&S need to maintain a high skill level among its staff.
3) Identifying skills required for future job assignments that would prepare employees to meet the corporation's challenges.

The center uses divisional employees as senior advisers. Advisers take an in-house class in administering as assessment and planning tool career called Career Anchors. The center enables IS&S staff to reach a clearer understanding of where their strengths lie and how they fit into the organization.

Gupta and Jenkins (1992) established, by using data from people who stayed with the job, who changed jobs, or who changed employers, the relative validity of three theoretical frameworks regarding the impact of turnover on perceived job quality. Data on 651 employees were obtained from two automotive suppliers and four service departments of a university hospital. Data from 272 employees of three of these organizations were collected about two years later. Respondents for whom data were available in both phases of the study were used in the analysis.

Despite the fact that that replacements and turnover had changed jobs or employers, these respondents tended not to see major improvements in their jobs or working conditions. Those who stayed saw more improvements in their financial rewards than did people who quit voluntarily and had been employed in a new job for a reasonable period of time (turnovers). For three facets (supervision, coworkers, and promotion opportunities), turnovers reported the greatest improvements: for three others (hours, effort, and fringe benefits), they report the greatest deterioration. Krishnaswamy (1993) in his study of employees' absenteeism discovered that promotional opportunity, salary satisfaction, immediate superior support, and job satisfaction are among the variables that have causal impact on voluntary absenteeism.

Besides looking at the above literature reviews related to the variables in this study, it is vital for us to look at studies of bank industry that had been carried out in overseas. As a matter of fact, sources of bank industry in Malaysia were very hard to be obtained due to lack of studies. However, there are many studies carried out in western countries, and therefore, generalizations of the previous studies to be applied in this study seem to be justifiable.

From the above literature, we could see that there were some studies of bank industry done in the western countries. In such a case, it is important for the study of bank industry to be carried out in Malaysia as well, so that these organizations could set their strategy and other management matters in a more cautious, effective, and efficient way.

2.6 Description of Variables and Conceptual Framework

Figure 2.1 represents the framework for this research study. The framework consists of three different types of variables, namely, independent, dependent, and moderating variables. There are three independent variables in this study. They are organizational empowerment and trust, career advancement opportunities, and job satisfaction. Gender, age, and educational level have been theorized as a moderating variable and finally organizational commitment is set as the dependent variable.

2.6.1 Justification of variables

Justification of each variable was provided in order to give a clearer picture on why each variable has a significant role to play in determining organizational commitment. These variables have been made up as the independent, dependent, and moderating variables due to their different important roles to play in predicting organizational commitment level. Their important role has been well supported by the literature review in Chapter 2 of this study, andtherefore they are the best predictors for measuring organizational commitment.

2.6.2 Independent Variables

There are three independent variables to be studied in this research paper. Definition of each variable would be defined as follows:

2.6.3 Organizational Empowerment and Trust

Organizational empowerment and trust can be defined as the employee has the access to information, receiving support, having access to resources necessary to do the job, and having opportunity to learn and grow. The importance to the growth of empowerment is having access to information, receiving support, having access to resources necessary to do the job, and having opportunity to learn and grow. Access to this empowering structure is facilitated by formal job characteristics. That is, jobs that are visible and central to the organization's goals and that allow the employee flexibility enhance empowerment.

Decreased organizational trust is associated with decrease communication and increase conflict. As this continues, employee trust and morale are eroded as workloads increase and job insecurity escalates. In such low trust organizations, behaviors such as high absenteeism, prolonged breaks, limited learning, low accountability, reactionary thinking, low creativity, and low productivity are predictably common.

2.6.4 Career Advancement Opportunities

Career advancement opportunities can be defined as a perception of how far an employee can pursue in his or her career and whether an employee has the chance to grow or advance his or her career in an organization. Yoong (1997) stated that what an employee needs is job security and the ability of the employer to provide greater opportunities for individual growth. Gaines (1994) found that one approach to keep employees dedicated and productive when traditional rewards cannot be given is to help employees take charge of their career advancement or development and job satisfaction.

2.6.5 Job satisfaction

One of most popular definition of job satisfaction is that the employees are happy with its current job and happy with what they are actually doing currently and their satisfaction that is derived from their engaged work.

Gaines (1994) and Yoong (1997) pointed that there may be several variables between people and their jobs that help to determine whether the relationship is satisfying. Among the factors are

- Expectations: whether an individual expects the job to be challenging and well compensated.
- Self-evaluation: an individual will look upon himself as a generally satisfied person.
- Social norms: the perception of others on the job that an individual is doing.
- Social comparison: comparison made with friends whether the friends are better off or otherwise.
- Input and output: job satisfaction can also be perceived on how individual put in his effort to achieve good results.
- Commitment: the sense of commitment that one feels when performing a job to his satisfaction.

Job satisfaction involves the satisfaction that is being derived from engaging in work. It is an attitude or an end feeling that the employee's experience after completed a task. From the literature review, employees who are happy with their job contribute in a more positive way toward organization. High job satisfaction leads to high productivity, low absenteeism, low turnover, and low rates of major health setbacks.

2.6.6 Dependent variables

2.6.7 Organizational commitment

There was only one dependent variable in this study and that would be organizational commitment. Organizational commitment is an appropriate question for those who are interested in organizational productivity and performance. Organizational commitment was made as a dependent variable explaining multiple dimensions of organizational effectiveness such as adaptability, turnover, productivity, and tardiness rate.

Organizational commitment is defined as the degree or a state in which an employee identifies with a particular organization and its goal and wishes to maintain membership in the organization, according to Robbin (1996). It is also a part of various job attitudes. Recently, the more global organizational commitment attitude that has emerged out of the research literature has been important to understanding and predicting organizational behavior, supported by Luthans (2007). Kanter (1968) explained the term "commitment" which is also been used, for example, to describe such diverged phenomena as the willingness of social actors to give their energy and loyalty to social system.

While Moon (2000) and Buchanan (1974) pointed an awareness of the impossibility of choosing a different social identity or of rejecting a particular expectation, under force of penalty or an affective attachment to an organization apart from the purely instrumental worth of the relationship. Organizational loyalty has been characterized as accepting organizational goals and policies, as mentioned by Johns (1996).

2.6.8 Moderating variables

The moderating variables in this study are age, gender, and educational level. These three variables become moderating variables because a contingency is created on the relationship between organizational empowerment and trust, job satisfaction, and career advancement opportunities on organizational commitment and therefore have interaction effect with the independent variables in explaining the variants. Bankers in this study are the employees who deal with administration, looking after process for improvement and assisting in improving the way of doing things in various departments within the bank.

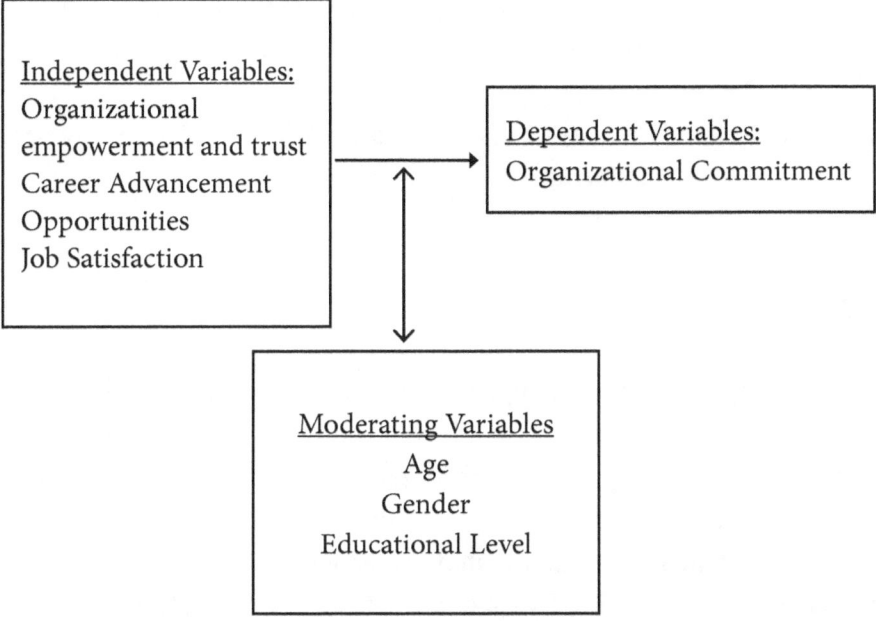

Figure 2.2: Conceptual Framework

Note. Solid lines indicate direct effects and double-headed arrows indicate moderating effects.

2.7 Development of Hypotheses

Based on the above findings and conceptual framework, the following hypotheses are developed:

Hypothesis 1: There will be a positive relationship between organizational empowerment and trust and organizational commitment.

Hypothesis 2: There will be a positive relationship between career advancement opportunities and organizational commitment.

Hypothesis 3: There will be a positive relationship between job satisfaction and organizational commitment.

Hypothesis 4: The above relationships are to be moderated by age, gender, and educational level.

2.8 Summary

The results of the studies suggested that different employees exhibit different levels of organizational commitment characteristics. This showed the differing degree of organizational empowerment and trust, job satisfaction, and career advancement opportunities among employees, which also moderated by gender, age, and educational level carried or possessed by each individual. Therefore, this study was focused on the relationship between organizational commitment with organizational empowerment and trust, job satisfaction, and career advancement opportunities.

In the following chapter, we would be looking at the methodology that is used in this research work, where the chapter would provide the definition of all the terms such as the independent variables, dependent variables, and moderating variables. Meanwhile, the purpose of the study and the population as well as the sample will be shown.

CHAPTER 3
Methodology

3.1 Introduction

The objective of this study was to measure the level of organizational commitment among bankers in Malaysia. This chapter described the type of study undertaken, sources of data, data collection techniques and data analysis techniques.

The research was based on a questionnaire survey seeking respondent's feedback on how they perceived the organizational commitment level within the organization that they engage their services. The respondents were required to review on their organizational empowerment and trust, job satisfaction, and career advancement opportunities in order to determine their commitment level.

This study was a basic of fundamental research. It was descriptive in nature and designed to describe characteristics of the population or a phenomenon. The main characteristics of the population addressed in this study were to determine the organizational commitment level among bankers in Malaysia.

3.2 Research Site, Population, and Sample

Data were collected from bankers employed by banks located in the states of Penang, Johor, and Wilayah Persekutuan, Malaysia. Initially, the geographical coverage was to be throughout Malaysia, but subsequently this intention was abandoned due to three major reasons. First was the setback in gathering information on bankers especially those located in the states of Perlis, Terengganu, and Kedah. In these three states, not only were records on foreign banks relatively limited but also the information obtained would have been inadequate to be representative of the states as two out of the three foreign banks approached refused to participate. Finally, most of the professional bankers from the less developed regions in Malaysia were relocating to the cities and bigger towns like Kuala Lumpur and Georgetown where career opportunities for bankers are greater and where the large local and foreign banks operate.

The states of Penang, Johor, and Wilayah Persekutuan were chosen as these are the states where most of the local and foreign banks are located in Malaysia including Citigroup, Standard Charted, OCBC, UOB and Bank of China and it was found that more than half of the professionals in these states originated from other states in Malaysia. This may suggest that the sample in Penang, Johor and Wilayah Persekutuan could be representative of the sample for Malaysia. In view of the above mentioned the decision to focus on Penang, Johor, and Wilayah Persekutuan rather than on all states in Malaysia seemed reasonable.

3.3 Purpose of the Study and the Population

The purpose of the study was to investigate the impact of organizational trust, career advancement opportunities, and job satisfaction on organizational commitment among employees (bankers) of the banks located in the states of Penang, Johor, and Wilayah Persekutuan, Malaysia. The research was based on a questionnaire survey seeking respondents' feedback on how they perceived their commitment level toward the organization that they are engaged to.

3.4 Sample

The listings of all bankers in the bank were obtained. It consisted of 900 bankers throughout the three states (each state thirty banks were chosen randomly). As many as 206 bankers in the three states completed and returned the questionnaire.

3.4.1 Justification of the samples

The targeted samples of this research were from the bank industry, and these samples were selected because they had been growing their business in a very aggressive way since their services started in Malaysia.

During the past two decades, some foreign banks were not available in Malaysia, but today in almost all the big town within the country, consumers can easily shop at the bank in a very different way compared to the way they used to consume in the minifinancial houses. According to Lai (2001), both local and foreign banks have been growing steadily in the country. Despite the high market growth, the bank industry still remains behind when compared to Kuala Lumpur where there are more than 56% banks, Kuala Lumpur being the capital of Malaysia. This is due to the late start of the bank industry in Penang and Johor, Malaysia.

Therefore, in order for both local and foreign banks to grow up to the level as achieved in Kuala Lumpur, it is crucial for the organizations to stay agile with the movement of the consumers, and of course to ensure that the employees' commitment level is high in order to strive for a better market share.

3.5 Questionnaire

3.5.1 Dependent Variable (IV)

Commitment to the organization is an attitude about employees' loyalty to their organization and is an ongoing process through which organizational participants express their concern for the organization and its continued success. Organizational commitment is the independent variable in this research. To measure organizational commitment, the questionnaire developed by Mowday, Steers, and Porter (1979) was used. It consisted of fifteen items, which were ranked by the respondents on the above-mentioned seven-point scale of agreement/disagreement.

3.5.2 Independent Variable (DV)

Organizational empowerment and trust—In order to measure the organizational empowerment, self-constructed was used to collect necessary data. The self-constructed questionnaire was used to measure four empowerments as described by Kanter—access to opportunity, information, support, and resources. These four subscales were each composed of four items based on a confirmatory factor analysis ranging from 4 to 20, higher score indicating higher perceived information, resources, and/ or opportunity. Items were derived from Kanter's original ethnographic study of work empowerment and trust.

Organizational trust—For the measurement of organizational trust, the interpersonal trust at work scale was used. This scale includes twelve-item instrument consisted of four subscales that would measure faith in the intentions of and confidence in actions of peers and managers. Items were summed and averaged to obtain scores ranging from 1 to 7 for each scale. The scales could be combined or used as separate measures of trust and confidence in management or peers.

Job satisfaction—The most common approach for measuring job satisfaction is the use of rating scales. To measure satisfaction, the Minnesota Satisfaction Questionnaire (MSQ) would be used. MSQ is one of the most popular ones developed by Sloan (1999). The questionnaire consisted of twenty items, which were answered by respondents on a seven-point scale ranging from very dissatisfied (1) to very satisfied (7).

Demographic questionnaire—Respondents were asked to indicate their age, gender, and educational level.

3.6 Data Collection Method

Questionnaires were distributed to the human resource manager for each of the bank in the sample. However, before the questionnaires were sent out, researcher was personally making phone calls to the human resource manager in seeking permission and was explaining to the person in charge about the purpose of the research conducted. Besides making phone calls, researcher did go to the targeted sample personally in order to explain to couple of the human resource management people.

At the same time, researcher also had to present his student ID card proving his identification as the student enrolled with the university. Several phone calls were made as a follow-up to ensure the human resource management people returning the questionnaire on time. Nevertheless, things were not going that smoothly as expected. The respond rates were not that high; finally researcher had to turn up again and extended the time frame from three to five weeks in order to ensure more questionnaires to be returned. After the fifth weeks, the questionnaires were collected personally.

3.7 Data Presentation and Analysis

After all data were collected and coded, then it was arranged in the file according to bankers from various states, then the whole information were saved in the computer for analysis.

In analyzing the data, SPSS program was used because the program is very friendly to use. SPSS program is data analysis software that contains many of the most common statistical analysis. Data analysis and presentation were guided by the purpose of study of this research paper. The objective was to measure the impact of organizational empowerment and trust, career advancement opportunities, and job satisfaction on organizational commitment for bankers. Details of the analysis would be further investigated in Chapter 4.

Cronbach's alpha was computed for all multiple questionnaire items to assess the reliability of the measure, which indicated consistency of respondents' answer to all the items in a measure. Item with low reliability measurement, i.e., Cronbach's alpha value of less than .5 would be dropped.

Prior to performing in-depth analysis on data gathered, descriptive analysis would be performed to understand profile of respondents and their organization. Statistics on gender, marital status, and education level would provide the researcher a good feel of the data gathered.

Correlate analysis would be held for testing the relationship between two continuous variables. For instance, job satisfaction and organizational commitment or vice versa, organizational empowerment and trust with career advancement opportunities or vice versa.

T-test was used in this research to determine whether a set or sets of scores are from the same population or not. Finally, when we wished to compare the means of more than two groups or levels of independent variables, a one-way analysis of variance (ANOVA) was needed to test on this.

3.8 Conclusion

In this chapter, the researcher had explained about the research model and the purpose of the study and the population. Justification of each component was presented followed by the explanation on the questionnaires and data collection method. Finally, the chapter also described on data presentation and analysis.

In the following chapter, we would look at how the SPSS program would be used in order to test the reliability and validity test for this study. Other than that, result for T-test, result for one-way ANOVA, and other analysis would be discussed and explained.

CHAPTER 4
Findings

4.1 Introduction

This chapter presented the survey findings and the results of statistical analysis. Firstly, the respondents and the bankers' characteristics of the bank industry in Penang, Johor, and Wilayah Persekutuan Kuala Lumpur, Malaysia, would be discussed. The next section would be the reliability of measurement and descriptive analysis of composite variable. Then, we would have the hypothesis testing. Finally, it would be the summary of the study.

4.2 Sample Characteristics

From the 900 questionnaires distributed, 206 responded (32.89% usable rate) within a time span of five weeks. The summary of sample profile is provided as follows:

Table 4.1: Sample Profile

Demographic Variable	Category	Frequency, N = 143	Percentage
a) Gender	Male	116	56.3
	Female	87	42.2
	Missing	3	1.5
b) Marital status	Married	88	42.7
	Single	101	49.0
	Divorced	8	3.9
	Widowed	2	1.0
	Missing	7	3.4
c) Education	High school	84	40.8
	Diploma	68	33.0
	Bachelor degree	40	19.4
	Postgraduate	5	2.4
	Missing	9	4.4

The characteristics could be distinctively described as follows and clearly be illustrated in the form of figures:—

a) 56.3% are male and 42.2% are female.
b) 42.7% are married, 49% are single, 3.9% are divorced, and 1% is widowed.
c) 40.8% are high school certificate holders, 33% are diploma holders, 19.4% are degree holders, and 1.9% is postgraduate degree holders.

Figure 4.1 Gender Profile of the Respondents

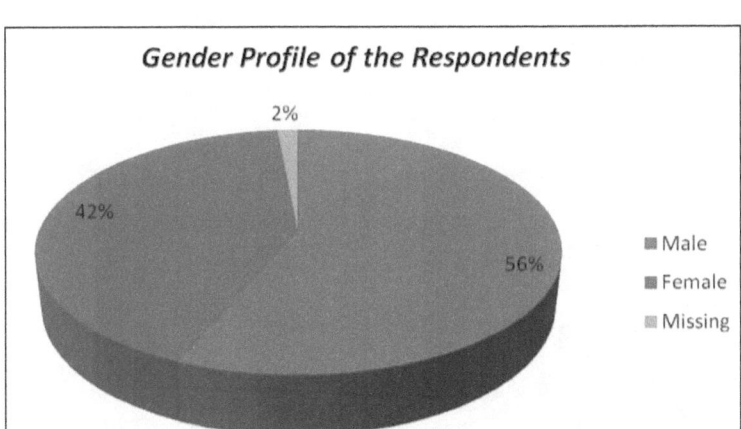

Figure 4.1 illustrates that 56% of the respondents were male, 42% were female, and 2% which is three respondents profile were missing

Figure 4.2 Marital Status of the Respondents

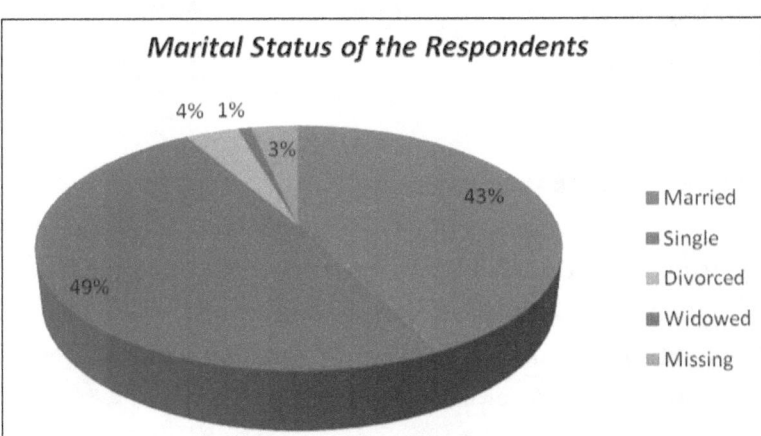

Figure 4.2 provided overall marital status of the respondents with the following breakdowns: 49% of the respondents were single, followed by 43% who were married. 4% and 1% were divorcees and widows, respectively, and 3% were missing values.

Figure 4.3 Educational Level of the Respondents

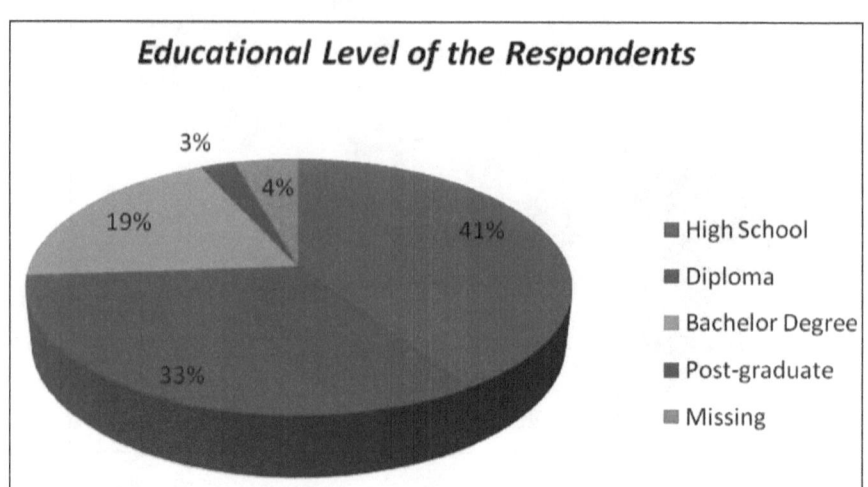

Figure 4.3 provided overall educational level of the respondents with the following findings: 41% of the respondents were equipped with high school diploma, 33% armed with diploma, 19% of 143 respondents had bachelor degree, and 3% with postgraduate degree with 3% of missing values.

4.3 Reliability Test

In order to ensure the reliability of the measures, the multiple statements on job satisfaction, organizational empowerment and trust, career advancement opportunities, and organizational commitment were assessed with Cronbach's alpha reliability test.

The reliability test was run to see if the items measuring the job satisfaction, organizational empowerment and trust, career advancement opportunities, and organizational commitment repetitively were internally consistent and if they could be added to obtain a single score for each of the variables.

The alpha value ranges from .8355 to .9316. The value of Cronbach's alpha indicated the high reliability of measurement for all the independent variables. Table 4.2 shows the alpha value for all variable grouping.

Table 4.2: Cronbach's Alpha Test

Variable	Questions	Cronbach's Alpha
Career advancement and opportunity	Part A Questions 2, 3, 5, 8, 10, 12, 13, 17, 18, 19, 30	.8888
Job satisfaction	All Part B Questions	.8355
Organizational commitment	All Part C Questions	.9316
Organizational empowerment and trust	All Part D Questions	.8688

4.4 Data Presentation

The three independent variables—organizational empowerment and trust, career advancement opportunities, and job satisfaction—were measured by using variables Part D questionnaires, Part A Questions 2, 3, 5, 8, 10, 12, 13, 17, 18, 19, and 30 and Part B Questionnaires. Whereas the dependent variable—organizational commitment—was measured by using variables Part C Questionnaires.

The cumulative results or findings are listed in Table 4.3.

Table 4.3: Cumulative Results

Variable	Mean	Std. Deviation	Min	Max	Valid
Career advancement and opportunity	2.8373	0.6711	1.45	4.55	206
Job satisfaction	3.2556	0.6922	0.30	4.70	206
Organization commitment	4.3575	1.1500	0.00	6.67	206
Organization empowerment and trust	3.5083	0.9322	0.00	5.00	206

In summary, the average responses for all four individual variables in their respective capacities were neutral, which were scored from 2.8 to 4.3. The standard deviations were small, indicating that the spread or dispersion was small. The cumulative correlation coefficients between the independent variables—organizational empowerment and trust, career advancement opportunities, and job satisfaction—as well as the dependent variable, denoted as organizational commitment respectively, are tabulated in Table 4.4.

Table 4.4: Correlation Coefficients

	JOBSAT	OC	OET
CAO	−0.6989 (195) $p = .000$	−0.7172 (195) $p = .000$	−0.7075 (195) $p = .000$
JOBSAT		0.7499 (195) $p = .000$	0.6112 (195) $p = .000$
OC			0.7163 (195) $p = .000$

Note: CAO = career advancement opportunity; JOBSAT = job satisfaction; OET = organizational empowerment and trust; OC = organizational commitment.

The explanations and interpretations are as follows:

Job satisfaction and organizational commitment were significantly correlated with each other with correlation coefficient value at .7499 and p value at .000 ($p < .05$). This meant the more satisfied was at his/her job places, the more commitment they were to the organization.

Meanwhile, job satisfaction as well as organizational empowerment and trust were significantly correlated with each other with correlation coefficient value at .6112 and p value at .000 ($p < .05$). Therefore, it meant that the more satisfied was at his/her job places, the more empowerment and trust they were to the organization.

At the same time, organizational commitment as well as organizational empowerment and trust were significantly correlated with each other with correlation coefficient value at .7163 and p value at .000 ($p < .05$). In such a case, this meant that the more his/her commitment, the more empowerment and trust they had to the organization.

The following (refer Tables 4.5.1, 4.5.2, 4.5.3, and 4.5.4) results are *T*-test results for gender, marital status, age, and education level in relation to job satisfaction, organization empowerment and trust, career advancement opportunity, and organizational commitment, respectively.

Table 4.5.1: Results of T-Test for Age

	Age	N	Mean	Std. Deviation	Sig.	Std. Error Mean
Career advancement and opportunity	≥35.00	67	2.3615	0.5129	.003	0.06266
	<35.00	137	3.0729	0.6165		0.05267
Job satisfaction	≥35.00	67	3.7657	0.5782	.316	0.07064
	<35.00	137	3.0204	0.5519		0.04715
Organizational commitment	≥35.00	67	5.3055	0.7922	.082	0.09679
	<35.00	137	3.9205	0.9541		0.08152
Organization empowerment and trust	≥35.00	67	4.1403	0.6147	.001	0.07510
	<35.00	137	3.2248	0.8708		0.07440

We could conclude the above result in Table 4.5.1 that irrespective of age difference among bankers, there were significant difference in their organization empowerment and trust, career advancement opportunity, and organization commitment. However, there was no significant difference in their job satisfaction.

Table 4.5.2: Results of T-Test for Gender

	Gender	N	Mean	Std. Deviation	Sig.	Std. Error Mean
Career advancement and opportunity	Male	116	2.8566	0.7326	.013	0.06802
	Female	87	2.8175	0.5912		0.06338
Job satisfaction	Male	116	3.2707	0.6860	.457	0.06369
	Female	87	3.2684	0.6409		0.06871

Organization commitment	Male	116	4.3614	1.2058	.028	0.1120
	Female	87	4.3846	0.9862		0.1057
Organization empowerment and trust	Male	116	3.5759	0.9338	.294	0.08670
	Female	87	3.4724	0.8634		0.09257

From Table 4.5.2, we could conclude that irrespective of gender difference among bankers, there are significant differences in their career advancement opportunity and organization commitment. Conversely, there was no significant difference in their job satisfaction as well as organization empowerment and trust.

Table 4.5.3: Results of *T*-Test for Marital Status

	Marital Status	N	Mean	Std. Deviation	Sig.	Std. Error Mean
Career advancement and opportunity	Married	88	2.5006	0.5035	.000	0.05367
	Single	101	3.1205	0.6822		0.06788
Job satisfaction	Married	88	3.5676	0.6058	.593	0.06458
	Single	101	2.9906	0.5929		0.05900
Organization commitment	Married	88	4.9947	0.9019	.491	0.09615
	Single	101	3.7545	0.9753		0.09705
Organization empowerment and trust	Married	88	3.9659	0.7073	.057	0.07539
	Single	101	3.2000	0.8993		0.08949

The conclusion for the above result in Table 4.5.3 was that irrespective of marital status difference among bankers, there was significant difference in career advancement opportunity. Nevertheless, there was no significant difference in their organization empowerment and trust, job satisfaction, and organization commitment.

Table 4.5.4: Results of T-Test for Educational Level

	Education Level	N	Mean	Std. Deviation	Sig.	Std. Error Mean
Career advancement and opportunity	≥2.50	45	2.4704	0.5905	.054	0.08803
	<2.50	152	2.9507	0.6671		0.05411
Job satisfaction	≥2.50	45	3.6244	0.5331	.048	0.07947
	<2.50	152	3.1599	0.6726		0.05455
Organization commitment	≥2.50	45	4.8269	1.1148	.218	0.1662
	<2.50	152	4.2230	1.0928		0.08863
Organization empowerment and trust	≥2.50	45	3.9289	0.8777	.572	0.1308
	<2.50	152	3.4237	0.8673		0.07035

We could conclude for the above result in Table 4.5.4 that irrespective of education level difference among bankers, there was significant difference in job satisfaction. Nonetheless, there was no significant difference in their organization empowerment and trust, career advancement opportunity, and organization commitment.

One-way ANOVA test was conducted on gender, educational level, marital status, and bankers of the respondents in relation to the four variables of organizational empowerment and trust, career advancement opportunities, job satisfaction, and organizational commitment.

The scores for the ANOVA tests are as follows:

Table 4.6.1: Results for One-Way ANOVA (Variables with Gender)

		Sum of Squares	df	Mean Square	F	Sig.
Career advancement and opportunity	Between groups	0.07593	1	0.07593	0.166	.684
	Within groups	91.780	201	0.457		
	Total	91.856	202			
Job satisfaction	Between groups	0.0002627	1	0.0002627	0.001	.981
	Within groups	89.441	201	0.445		
	Total	89.441	202			
Organization commitment	Between groups	0.02680	1	0.02680	0.021	.884
	Within groups	250.836	201	1.248		
	Total	250.863	202			
Organization empowerment and trust	Between groups	0.532	1	0.532	0.651	.421
	Within groups	164.386	201	0.818		
	Total	164.918	202			

Table 4.6.2: Results for One-Way ANOVA (Variables with Marital Status)

		Sum of Squares	df	Mean Square	F	Sig.
Career advancement and opportunity	Between groups	18.234	3	6.078	16.611	.000
	Within groups	71.352	195	0.366		
	Total	89.586	198			
Job satisfaction	Between groups	16.929	3	5.643	15.380	.000
	Within groups	71.549	195	0.367		
	Total	88.478	198			
Organization commitment	Between groups	79.764	3	26.588	30.691	.000
	Within groups	168.932	195	0.866		
	Total	248.696	198			
Organization empowerment and trust	Between groups	27.984	3	9.328	14.150	.000
	Within groups	128.551	195	0.659		
	Total	156.535	198			

Table 4.6.3: Results for One-Way ANOVA (Variables with Education Level)

		Sum of Squares	df	Mean Square	F	Sig.
Career advancement and opportunity	Between groups	21.390	3	7.130	19.897	.000
	Within groups	69.163	193	0.358		
	Total	90.554	196			
Job satisfaction	Between groups	20.182	3	6.727	19.060	.000
	Within groups	68.120	193	0.353		
	Total	88.302	196			
Organization commitment	Between groups	50.647	3	16.882	16.539	.000
	Within groups	197.006	193	1.021		
	Total	247.653	196			
Organization empowerment and trust	Between groups	47.996	3	15.999	28.497	.000
	Within groups	108.353	193	0.561		
	Total	156.349	196			

Table 4.6.4: Results for One-Way ANOVA (Variables with Executive vs. Nonexecutive)

		Sum of Squares	df	Mean Square	F	Sig.
Career advancement and opportunity	Between groups	25.336	1	25.336	76.970	.000
	Within groups	64.187	195	0.329		
	Total	89.522	196			
Job satisfaction	Between groups	17.435	1	17.435	48.580	.000
	Within groups	69.982	195	0.359		
	Total	87.416	196			
Organization commitment	Between groups	56.609	1	56.609	58.488	.000
	Within groups	188.736	195	0.968		
	Total	245.344	196			
Organization empowerment and trust	Between groups	57.720	1	57.720	113.906	.000
	Within groups	98.813	195	0.507		
	Total	156.532	196			

From the result presented in Table 4.6.1, we found out that there were insignificant in terms of gender with four variables, which are organizational commitment, organizational empowerment and trust, career advancement opportunities, and job satisfaction. Whereas from the second result in Table 4.6.2, in terms of marital status with four variables, it indicated that the marital status was significant with the organizational commitment, organizational empowerment and trust, career advancement opportunities, and job satisfaction.

On the other hand, we found out for the third result in Table 4.6.3 that the education level was significant with the organizational commitment, organizational empowerment and trust, career advancement and opportunities, and job satisfaction.

However, for the last result in Table 4.6.4, it showed that the bankers versus nonbankers were significant with the organizational commitment, organizational empowerment and trust, career advancement opportunities, and job satisfaction.

4.5 Conclusions

The results of the findings from Table 4.1 showed that 56.3% are male and 42.2% are female. While from the total respondents, 42.7% are married, 49% are single, 3.9% are divorced, and 1% is widowed. Besides that, 40.8% are high school certificate holders, 33% are diploma holders, 19.4% are degree holders, and 1.9% are postgraduate degree holders.

From Table 4.3, the average responses for all four individual variables in their respective capacities were neutral, which were scored from 2.8 to 4.3. The standard deviations were small, indicating that the spread or dispersion was small.

From Table 4.4, job satisfaction and organizational commitment were significantly correlated with each other with correlation coefficient value at .7499 and p value at .000 ($p < .05$). This meant the more satisfied was at his/her job places, the more commitment they were to the organization.

At the same Table 4.4, we could discover that job satisfaction as well as organizational empowerment and trust were significantly correlated with each other with correlation coefficient value at .6112 and p value at 0.000 ($p < .05$). This meant the more satisfied was at his/her job places, the more empowerment and trust they were to the organization.

We could conclude in the same Table 4.4 that organizational commitment as well as organizational empowerment and trust were significantly correlated with each other with correlation coefficient value at .7163 and p value at .000 ($p < .05$). This meant the more commitment in his/her, the more empowerment and trust they were to the organization.

From Table 4.5.1, we concluded that irrespective of age difference among bankers, there were significant differences in their organization empowerment and trust, career advancement opportunity, and organization commitment. However, there was no significant difference in their job satisfaction.

Referring to Table 4.5.2 for gender difference among bankers, there were significant differences in their career advancement opportunity and organization commitment. Conversely, there was no significant difference in their job satisfaction as well as organization empowerment and trust.

For marital status difference among bankers from Table 4.5.3, there was significant difference in career advancement opportunity. Nevertheless, there was no significant difference in their organization empowerment and trust, job satisfaction, and organization commitment.

Meanwhile for education level difference among bankers from Table 4.5.4, there was significant difference in job satisfaction. Nonetheless, there was no significant difference in their organization empowerment and trust, career advancement opportunity, and organization commitment.

CHAPTER 5
Conclusions

5.1 Background

The main purpose of this study was to examine the impact of organizational commitment on bankers in Malaysia. A significant relationship between the dependent variables, independent variable, and moderating variables was determined. A comparison had been made among the variables to identify the impact of organizational commitment in the bank industry. In addition, the feedbacks of human resource managers had been obtained to determine the employees' commitment level.

As the results obtained in Chapter 4, various findings were found. The summary of the findings was shown in the following paragraphs.

5.2 Summary of Findings

In Table 5.1, the cell with the "+" and "−" showed that there is relationship among the dependent variable, independent variables, and moderating variables. The "+" indicated that the relationship was high commitment to the organizational commitment, whereas

"–" indicated that the relationship was low commitment to the organizational commitment.

Table 5.1: Findings Summary

Dependent Variables	Independent Variables	Positive (+)	Negative (–)
Organizational commitment	Organizational empowerment and trust	+	
	Career advancement opportunities	+	
	Job satisfaction	+	
	Moderating Variables		
	Age	+	
	Gender		–
	Educational level		–

Organizational trust and empowerment have significant relationship with organizational commitment. From the result, it supported that the organizational trust and empowerment have a significant role to play in organizational commitment. The higher the organizational trust and empowerment the employee has, the higher will be the organizational commitment. In another words, the more trust and empowerment an employee possess in order for them to carry out their duty, the more committed they are toward the organization.

Career advancement opportunities also have a significant relationship through the finding. The correlation result shows that the employees who have the positive view toward career advancement opportunities tend to be more committed. This means that the higher the opportunity for career advancement, the higher the organizational commitment will be. However, the career advancement opportunities must be appropriately carried out because some employees tend to stay at their current position even though they have the opportunity to be promoted. This is because some employees who are strong in the technical background can find it to be quite uneasy if they are going to handle different things such as paper work and supervision without handling technical stuff. Thus, it is very important to note that even though through the finding we can see the direct relationship of career advancement opportunities and organizational commitment, it still has to be monitored closely and each employee's perception must be known before they are actually promoted.

The finding also showed that job satisfaction has a positive relationship with organizational commitment. The higher the job satisfaction of an employee, the higher will be the organizational commitment toward the organization. Therefore, it is important for the organization to know that employees' satisfaction in their job tend to be more committed and it is advisable to ensure that employees are satisfied with their job. If the employees are not satisfied with their job, the organization has to quickly find out why they are not satisfied. From there the organization must find way and think of what can be done in order to ensure the employees stay satisfied with their job and more importantly commit to the organization because good employees are hard to find and people are the greatest assets in any organization.

After looking at the relationship between dependent variable and independent variable, we would move on to look at how the moderating variables play their role in order to enhance the organizational commitment.

Age is one of the moderating variables in this study. From the finding, it is shown that commitment level of an employee increases with their age. This means that the older the employee, the higher will be the commitment level toward the organization. This is due so because through the interview with the human resource manager, researcher was told that the turnover rate of the older employee is lower compared to the younger one and older employee also tend to be more satisfied with their job and not intend to practice job hopping and older employees may find comfortable and have lesser expectation. Besides that, they are also aware that they have limited choice probably because they cannot find other job easily or have no skill to match the job available in the market.

Gender is another moderating variable in determining organizational commitment in this study. From the finding it is shown that females tend to be more committed to the organization compared to males. It may be because the job at the bank is more of feminine type and that is why females are more committed.

The last moderating variable in this study is the educational level. The finding showed that the higher the educational levels of the employees, the lesser the employees are committed toward the organization. This is because the higher the educational level the employee has, the individual tend to be more demanding and they think that they have a better option compared to their current job. Besides that, they also have the thinking that they can easily get a job because they have the qualification and they are always looking for a more challenging career and expecting more than those received lesser qualification.

5.3 Recommendations

From the findings above, we could see there were many positive relationships among the dependent variables, independent variable, and moderating variables. After looking at the findings, some relevant recommendations were made as below.

5.3.1 Recruitment of Older Employees

Since older employees seem to be more committed, the organization could plan on hiring more mature employees in future. However, this might be construed as discriminatory and adverse consequences might follow. Hence, this is not recommended. In any case, for the more responsible positions such as managers of the various departments, only the more experienced members are hired, this is one of the ways to enhance organizational commitment.

5.3.2 Enhancing Job Satisfaction

As discussed earlier, enhancing job satisfaction of employees can increase organizational commitment. Besides looking at customers' needs, the organizations must also take care of employees' needs. In addition, the organization must make sure its employees are satisfied with their job and working environment in order to increase the level of organizational commitment. One of the ways may be superior-subordinate relationship. This might be an excellent way because when the superior and the subordinate are working hand in hand, both parties are more satisfied with his or her job. In such a case, the relationship of superior and subordinate is vital in making the job carried out smoothly.

5.3.3 Clear Career Advancement Opportunities

As we could see from the earlier discussion, career advancement opportunities have a positive relationship with organizational commitment. Thus, it is important for the organization to make it clear that employees have the opportunity to move up the ladder of the organization based on their performance or seniority. The organization can boost the morale of employees at all levels by paying attention to them. By taking rounds at various times a day, the department manager can discuss with the employees to show their concern and give compliment when things are proceeding smoothly, offer "employee of the month" awards based on some prespecified criteria of performance and so on. Though monetary incentives help, nonfinancial strategies such as the ones specified above also work just as effectively.

5.3.4 Increasing Trust and Empowerment

While for this case, it is recommended to expand the job scope or responsibilities for personnel doing routine jobs. For instance, the cash counter employees, the purchasers, staff of the various departments including the managers, and the cashiers and accountants can be given a lot of freedom to plan and organize their work themselves. By giving these individuals more responsibility to handle their work, it means that trust and empowerment are increased. Therefore, this will also result in increasing organizational commitment.

5.4 Implications

In conclusion, this research proved that the independent variables (organizational empowerment and trust, career advancement opportunities, and job satisfaction) and moderating variables (age, gender, and educational level) did predict organizational commitment level of the bankers in Penang, Johor, and Wilayah Persekutuan Kuala Lumpur, Malaysia. Therefore, some implications that needed top management include (1) developing processes by which cooperative rather than competitive interactions are encouraged among all employees; (2) building more autonomy into the jobs of bankers; (3) evaluating the effectiveness of duty that assigned; (4) having training sessions for all those who supervise others in effective interpersonal relationships; and (5) developing criteria for recognizing and rewarding employees with superior performance.

5.5 Limitation of the Study

This study had its own limitation due to some restrictions. The following are the limitations, which may influence the findings of the study:

a) This study was oriented to bankers in Malaysia only. Therefore, the findings might not hold true for health-care employees or other categories of employees of other sector.
b) The sample only consisted of the bankers in Penang, Johor, and Wilayah Persekutuan Kuala Lumpur, Malaysia. Data collected from other state might differ due to the working climate and therefore generalization to other organizations might be limited.
c) Organizational commitment was not only to be determined by factors such as organizational empowerment and trust, job satisfaction, and career advancement opportunities, and therefore there might be other factors that affect organizational commitment

5.6 Suggestion for Future Research

Since this research covers only bankers in Penang, Johor, and Wilayah Persekutuan Kuala Lumpur, Malaysia, it was suggested that the future study should also include the top management employees in order to measure both current and future results are true and matched.

The future research should also study other independent variables such as leadership, coworkers relationship, working environment, and other fringe benefits that can contribute to organizational commitment.

This study limited itself to three independent variables—organizational empowerment and trust, career advancement opportunities, and job satisfaction. Organizational commitment is a function of a host of other variables, which should be examined in future research.

REFERENCES

Allen, N. J., and J. P. Meyer. 1990. "The Measurement and Antecedents of Affective, Continuance and Normative Commitment to the Organization." *Journal of Occupational Psychology* 63: 1-18.

Angle, H. L., and J. L. Perry. 1981. "An Empirical Assessment of Organizational Commitment and Organizational Effectiveness." *Administrative Science Quarterly* 26: 1-14.

Aven, F. F., B. Parker, and G. M. McEvoy. 1993. "Gender and Attitudinal Commitment to Organizations: A Meta-Analysis." *Journal of Business Research* 26: 63-73.

Ayupp, K., and M. N. Tiong. 2011. "A Study of Workplace Stress and Its Relationship with Job Satisfaction Among Officers in the Malaysian Banking Sector." *Interdisciplinary Journal of Contemporary* 403-17.

Balfour, D. L., and B. Wechsler. 1996. "Organizational Commitment: Antecedents and Outcomes in Public Organizations." *Public Productivity and Management Review* 29: 256-77.

Becker, H. S. 1960. "Notes on the Concept of Commitment." *American Journal of Sociology* 66: 32-40.

Behrman, D. N., and W. D. Perrcault. 1984. "A Role Stress Model of the Performance and Satisfaction of Industrial Salesperson." *Journal of Marketing* 48: 9-21.

Benkhoff, B. 1997. "Ignoring Commitment Is Costly: New Approaches Establish the Missing Link Between Commitment and Performance." *Human Relations* 50: 702-27.

Benson, T. E. 1991. "Empowerment: There Is That Word Again." *Industry Week* 240(9): 44-52.

Bowen, W., and Q. Lawler. 1992. "The Empowerment of Service Workers: What, Why, How and When." *Sloan Management Review* 25(4): 31-9.

Buchanan, B. 1974. "Building Organizational Commitment: The Socialization of Managers in Work Organizations." *Administrative Science Quarterly* 19: 530-46.

Byham, S. 1992. "Would You Recognize An Empowered Organization if You Saw One?" *Tapping the Network Journal* 3(2): 10-3.

Cherniss, C. 1991. "Career Commitment in Human Service Professionals: A Biographical Study." *Human Relations* 44: 419-37.

Cohen, A. 1992. "Antecedents of Organizational Commitment Across Occupational Groups: A Meta-Analysis." *Journal of Organizational Behavioral* 13: 539-58.

Colbert, A. E., and I. G. Kwon. 2000. "Factors Related to the Organizational Commitment of College and University Auditors." *Journal of Managerial Issues*.

Cook, J., and T. Wall. 1980. "New Work Attitude Measures of Trust, Organizational Commitment, and Personal Need Fulfillment." *Journal of Occupational Psychology* 53: 39-52.

Conger, J. A., and R. N. Kanungo. 1988. "The Empowerment Process: Integrating Theory and Practice." *Academy of Management Review* 13: 471-82.

Curry, J. P., D. S. Wakefield, J. L. Price, and C. W. Mueller. 1986. "On the Causal Ordering of Job Satisfaction and Organizational Commitment." *Academy of Management Journal* 29: 847-58.

Deakin, D., and Boussouara, M. 2000. "Trust and the Acquisition of Knowledge from Non-executive Directors by High Technology Entrepreneurs." *International Journal of Entrepreneurial Behavior & Research* 6: 204-26.

Dillard, J. F., and K. R. Ferris. 1979. "Source of Professional Staff Turnover in Public Accounting Firms: Some Empirical Evidence." *Accounting, Organization, and Society* 4: 179-86.

Dunham, R. B., J. A. Grube, and M. B. Castaneda. 1994. "Organizational Commitment: The Utility of an Integrative Definition." *Journal of Applied Psychology* 79: 370-80.

Enriquez, Vicki, Jim McBride, and Liz Paxton. 2001. "Improving Knowledge of Strategic Goals and the Impact on Organizational Commitment." *Health Marketing Quarterly*.

Forsyth, P. 1995. "101 Ways to be a Better Time Manager." *Heinaman Asia*, Singapore.

Gaines, H. 1994. "Employees Get Satisfaction, But Only When Properly Motivated." *Industrial Management* 36(5): 2-3

Gilber, J. A., and L. P. T. Tang. 1998. "An Examination of Organizational Trust Antecedents." *Public Personnel Management* 27: 321-5.

Gupta, N., and G. D. Jenkins. 1992. "The Effects of Turnover on Perceived Job Quality: Does the Grass Look Greener?" *Group and Organizational Management* 17(4): 431-45.

Hackman, J. R., and G. IL Oldham. 1975. "Development of the Job Diagnostic Survey." *Journal of Applied Psychology* 60: 159-70.

Harrell, A. 1990. "A Longitudinal Examination of Large CPA Firm Auditors' Personnel Turnover." *Advanced in Accounting* 8: 233-46.

Heather, K., S. Laschinger, J. Finegan, and J. Shamian. 2001. "The Impact of Workplace Empowerment, Organizational Trust on Staff Nurses' Work Satisfaction and Organization Commitment." *Health Care Management Review.*

Henkin, A. B., and D. M. Marchiori. 2003. "Empowerment and Organizational Commitment of Chiropractic Faculty." *Journal of Manipulative and Physiological Therapeutics* 275-81.

Hrebiniak, L. G., and J. A. Alutto. 1972. "Personal and Role-Related Factors in the Development of Organizational Commitment." *Administrative Science Quarterly* 17: 555-73.

Johns, J. 1996. "A Concept Analysis of Trust." *Journal of Advanced Nursing* 24: 76-83.

Kanter, R. M. 1968. "Commitment and Social Organization: A Study of Commitment Mechanisms in Utopian Communities." *American Sociological Review* 33: 499-517.

Kanter, R. M. 1977. Men and Women of the Corporation. New York: *Basic Books*.

Kimbell, R. D., and S. Stonestreet. 2000. *Is Employee Loyalty Really Dead? What Are the Causes? Can Employee Loyalty be Revived?* Paper presented at the IBAM Conference, San Diego, California.

Kirkman, B. L., and D. L. Shapiro. 2001. "The Impact of Cultural Values on Job Satisfaction and Organizational Commitment in Self Managing Work Teams." *Academy of Management Journal.*

Kramer, M., and C. Schmalenberg. 1993. "Learning From Success: Autonomy and Empowerment." *Nursing Management* 25(5): 58-64.

Kramer, R. M., M. B. Brewer, and B. A. Hanna. 1993. "Collective Trust and Collection Action: The Decisions to Trust as a Social Decision." In *Trust in Organizations: Frontiers of Theory and Research*, edited by R. M. Kramer and T. R. Tyler, 357-89.

Krishnaswamy, S. "Causal Model of Employee Absenteeism: An Empirical Test" (Absenteeism, Voluntary Absenteeism). PhD diss., University of Iowa, 1993.

Leonard, B. 2000. Employee Loyalty Continues to Wane. *HR Magazine* 21-2.

Li, N. 2000. "The Perceived Leadership Behavior and Organizational Commitment at CPA Firms." *Management Project Presented*, Nova Southeastern University, FL.

Lu, L., and C. Shiau. (March, 1997). Occupational stress in clinical stress nurses. Counseling Psychology Quarterly. Available at: http://www.ebscohost.com.eserv.uum.edu.my/cgi-bin/epwbird.

Luthans, F. 2007. *Organizational Behavior*. New York: McGraw-Hill.

Macan, T. H. 1994. "Time Management: Test of Process Model." *Journal of Applied Psychology* 79 (3): 381-91

Maccoby, M. 1988. *Why Work?* New York: Simon and Schuster Inc.

Marsh, R. M., and H. Mannari. 1977. "Organizational Commitment and Turnover: A Prediction Study." *Administrative Science Quarterly* 22: 57-75.

Mathieu, A., Bruvold, N. T., and P. N. Ritchey. 2000. "Sub-Cultural Research on Organizational Commitment with the 15 OCQ Invariant Instruments." *The Journal of Personal Selling and Sales Management* 20: 129-38.

Mathieu, J. E., and D. M. Zajac. 1990. "A Review and Meta-Analysis of the Antecedents, Correlates, and Consequences of Organizational Commitment." *Psychological Bulletin* 108: 171-94.

McDaniel, C., and L. Stumpf. 1993. "The Organizational Culture: Implication for Nursing Science." *Journal of Nursing Administration* 23(4): 54-60.

Meyer, J. P., and N. J. Allen. 1991. "A Three-Component Conceptualization of Organizational Commitment." *Human Resource Management* 1: 61-89.

Mishra, A. K., and G. M. Spreitzer. 1988. "Explaining How Survivors Respond to Downsizing: The Roles of Trust, Empowerment, Justice and Work Redesign." *Academy of Management Review* 23: 567-88.

Moon, M. J. 2000. "Organizational Commitment Revisited in New Public Management." *Public Performance & Management Review*.

Morrow, P. C. 1983. "Concept Redundancy in Organizational Research: The Case of Work Commitment." *Academy of Management Review* 8: 486-500.

Mosadeghrad A. M. 2003. *Principles of Health Care Administration.* Tehran: Dibagran Tehran.

Mottaz, C. 1986. "Gender Differences in Work Satisfaction, Work Related Rewards and Values, and the Determinants of Work Satisfaction." *Human Relations* 39: 358-78.

Mowday, R. T. 2000. Chickens, Pigs, Breakfast, and Commitment. *OB News: Organizational Behavior Division of the Academy of Management*, 3.

Mowday, R. T., L. W. Porter, and R. M. Steers. 1982. *Employee-Organization Linkages: The Psychology of Commitment, Absenteeism, and Turnover.* New York: Academic Press.

Mowday, R. T., R. M. Steers, and L. W. Porter. 1979. "The Measurement of Organizational Commitment." *Journal of Vocational Behaviour* 14: 224-27.

Murry, M. A. and T. Atkinson. 1981. "Gender Differences in Correlates of Job Satisfaction." *Canadian Journal of Behavioral Science* 13: 44-52.

Narvan. 1992. "Empowerment Employees to Excel." *Supervisory Management* 32(5): 45-52.

Okpara, J. O. 2004. "Personal Characteristics as Predictors of Job Satisfaction: An Exploratory Study of IT Managers in a Developing Economy." *Information Technology & People* 17(3): 327-38.

Painter, J. A. 1994. "Relative Importance of Extrinsic and Intrinsic Rewards as Predictors of Job Satisfaction among Occupational Therapists in Ambulatory Care Setting." PhD diss., North Carolina State University.

Podsakoff, P. M., S. B. MacKenzie, and W. H. Bommer. 1996. "Transformational Leadership Behaviours and Substitutes For Leadership as Determinants of Employee Satisfaction, Commitment, Trust and Organizational Citizenship Behaviors." *Journal of Management* 22: 259-98.

Porter, L. W., R. Steers, M. Mowday, and R. Boulin. 1974. "Organizational Commitment, Job Satisfaction, and Turnover among Psychiatric Technicians." *Journal of Applied Psychology* 54(3): 603-9.

Quarles, R. 1994. "An Examination of Promotion Opportunities and Evaluation Criteria as Mechanisms for Affecting Bankers' Commitment, Job Satisfaction and Turnover Intentions." *Journal of Managerial Issues* 6: 176-94.

Quinn, R. P., G. Staines, and M. McCullough. 1974. *Job Satisfaction: Is There a Trend?* Washington, D.C.: U.S. Department Of Labor.

Robbins, S. P. 1996. *Organizational Behavior—Concepts, Controversies and Application.* 7th edition, New Jersey: Prentice Hall.

Saiyadain. M. S. 1985. "Personal Characteristics and Job Satisfaction: India-Nigeria Comparison." *International Journal of Psychology* 20: 143-53.

Shaw, J. D., J. E. Delery, and M. H. A. Abdulla. 2003. "Organizational Commitment and Performance Among Guest Workers and Citizens of an Arab Country." *Journal of Business Research* 56: 1021-30.

Sidle, S. D. 2003. "Best Laid Plans: Establishing Fairness Early Can Help Smooth Organizational Change." *Academy of Management Executive* 17: 127-9.

Sloan, C. 1999. Look Out for No. 2. *Home Textiles Today*, High Point.

Sommer, S., M. Bae, and F. Luthens. 1996. "Organizational Commitment Across Cultures: The Impact of Antecedents on Korean Employees." *Human Relations* 49: 997-993.

Spector, P. E. 1986. "Perceived Control by Employees. A Meta-Analysis of Studies Concerning Autonomy and Participation at Work." *Human Relations* 39(11): 1005-6.

Stanley, T. L. 2001. *The Joy of Working: A New Look at Job Satisfaction*. Burlington: Supervision.

Steers, R. M. 1977. "Antecedents and Outcomes of Organizational Commitment." *Administrative Science Quarterly* 22: 45-56.

Still, L. V. 1983. "Part-Time vs. Full-Time Salespeople: Individual Attributes, Organizational Commitment, and Work Attitudes." *Journal of Retailing* 59: 55-79.

Tella, A., C. O. Ayeni, and S. O. Popoola. 2007. "Work Motivation, Job Satisfaction and Organisational Commitment of Library Personnel in Academic and Research libraries in Oyo State, Nigeria." *Library Philosophy and Practice* 1-16.

Thomas, K. W., and B. A. Velthouse. 1990. "Cognitive Elements of Empowerment: An 'Interpretive' Model of Intrinsic Task Motivation." *Academy of Management Review* 15(4): 666-81.

Van Vianen, A. E. M., and A. H. Fischer. 2002. "Illuminating the Glass Ceiling: The Role of Organizational Culture Preferences." *Journal of Occupational and Organizational Psychology* 75: 315-37.

Vollmer, J. J., and J. A. Kinney. 1955. "Age, Education, and Job Satisfaction." *Personnel* 32: 39-43.

Wiener, Y., and A. S. Gechman. 1977. "Commitment: A Behavioral Approach to Job Involvement." *Journal of Vocational Behavior* 10: 47-52.

Woolridge, A. (2000, March 5). *Come Back, Company Man!* New York: Times Magazine, 82.

Yoong, M. H. 1997. "The Impact of Time Management on Job Satisfaction and Commitment to Organization." *Management Project Presented* at the University Sains Malaysia.

Zimmerman, M. A. 1995. "Psychology Empowerment: Issues and Illustrations." *American Journal of Community Psychology* 23: 581-600.

APPENDIX A
Questionnaire

Dear Respondent:

This is purely an academic exercise that is intended to examine organizational commitment specifically in financial-related industries. This has been undertaken to fulfill the requirement of the degree of Masters of Business Administration at the University of Derby. Please complete the questionnaire based on your honest opinion. Some of the questions may seem similar to each other, but each question addresses a unique issue. There is no right or wrong answer. We are mainly interested in your opinion.

All information provided by you will be kept strictly confidential and the name of the individual or organization is not required. All information provided by you will be used only for the purpose of this academic research. Your kind participation and assistance is highly appreciated in making this study successful.

Thank you for taking time off from your busy schedule to participate in this study. Should you have any queries or if you are interested to know the outcome of this study, please do not hesitate to contact my academic supervisors or me.

Many thanks for your valuable time, assistance, and support in completing this questionnaire.

Yours sincerely,

Kelechikwu Emmanuel Oguejiofor
UoD Index no: 100271210
MBA Student
E-mail: O.Kelechikwu-Emmanuel1@unimail.derby.ac.uk

Lecturer's Name: Dr Carlton
Position: Module Research Coordinator
E-mail: dr.carlton@hotmail.com

DERBYSHIRE BUSINESS SCHOOL: UNIVERSITY OF DERBY

Section 1

Please read the following statements carefully and indicate your agreement/disagreement with them on the space provided at the right hand side.

	This organization	1 Strongly Disagree	2 Disagree	3 Slightly Disagree	4 Neutral	5 Slightly Agree	6 Agree	7 Strongly Agree
1	Makes sure people have the resources they need to do a good job							
2	Rewards people fairly for their efforts							
3	Pays close attention to what others say							
4	Respects people's differences							
5	Creates opportunities for people to succeed							
6	Considers how a specific plan of action might be extended to benefit others							
7	Provides information people need to effectively plan and do their work							
8	Recognizes good performance with rewards people value							
9	Follows through on commitments							
10	Designs situations that permit people to achieve their goals							
11	Concentrates on clear and short-term goals							

12	Helps people get the training they need to perform their jobs effectively							
13	Expresses appreciation when people perform well							
14	Keeps promises							
15	Shows concern for the feelings of others							
16	Involves others in new ideas and projects							
17	Explains long-range plans and goals clearly							
18	Supports and encourages people to get the job done well							
19	Knows the rewards people value							
20	Listens for feelings as well as ideas							
21	Treats others with respect, regardless of position							
22	Helps others learn from mistakes							
23	Encourages people to support their views and positions with concrete evidence							
24	Makes sure people have clear and challenging goals							
25	Makes sure that people know what to expect in return for accomplishing goals							
26	Is able to get complicated ideas across clearly							
27	Can be trusted							
28	Makes others feel a real part of the group organization							
29	Gives people the authority they need to fulfill their responsibilities							
30	Has plans that extend over a period of several years or longer							

Section 2

Please read the following statements carefully and indicate your agreement/disagreement with them on the space provided at the left-hand side.

Please use the following scheme.

	On my present job, this is how I feel about	1 Strongly Disagree	2 Disagree	3 Slightly Disagree	4 Neutral	5 Slightly	6 Agree	7 Strongly Agree
1	Being able to keep busy all the time							
2	The chance to work alone on the job							
3	The chance to do different things from time to time							
4	The chance to be "somebody" in the community							
5	The way my boss handles the staff							
6	The competence of my supervisor in making decisions							
7	Being able to do things that don't go against my conscience							
8	The way my job provides for steady employment							
9	The chance to do things for other people							
10	The chance to tell people what to do							
11	The chance to do something that makes use of my abilities							
12	The way company policies are put into practice							

13	My pay and the amount of work I do							
14	The chances for advancement on this job							
15	The freedom to use my own judgment							
16	The chance to try my own methods of doing the job							
17	The working conditions							
18	The way my coworkers get along with each other							
19	The praise I get for doing a good job							
20	The feelings of accomplishment I get from the job							

Section 3

Following are a list of statements that relate to the degree of your feelings towards your organization. Please indicate the degree of your agreement or disagreement with each statement.

Please tick (√) the number of your choice for each statement based on the scale given below:

	Below are the statements of how people feel about the organizations in which they work. Please circle the appropriate number on the scale of 1 to 7 which most closely matches how you feel about your firm.	1 Strongly Disagree	2 Disagree	3 Slightly Disagree	4 Neutral	5 Slightly Agree	6 Agree	7 Strongly Agree
1	I am willing to put in a great deal of effort beyond what is normally expected in order to help this firm be successful							
2	I talk about this organization to my friends as a great firm to work for							

3	I feel very little loyalty to this firm								
4	I would accept almost any type of job assignment in order to keep working for this firm								
5	I find that my values and the firm's value are very similar								
6	I am proud to tell others that I am part of this firm								
7	I could just as well be working for a different firm as long as the type of work was similar								
8	This firm really inspires my best job performance								
9	It would take very little change in my present circumstances to cause me to leave this firm								
10	I am extremely glad that I chose this firm to work for over others I was considering at the time I joined								
11	There is not too much to be gained by sticking with this firm indefinitely								
12	Often, I find it difficult to agree with this firm's policies on important matters relating to its employees								
13	I really care about the fate of this firm								
14	For me, this is the best of all possible firms for which to work								
15	Decision to work for this firm was a definite mistake on my part								

Section 4

Instructions:

Please think about your organization (that is, your department) and respond to each statement below using one of the six choices in the scale shown below. Please enter your response in the space provided to the left of each statement.

	Please think about your organization (that is, your department) and respond to each statement below using one of the six choices in the scale shown below. Please enter your response in the space provided to the left of each statement.	1 Almost Never	2 Rarely	3 Sometimes	4 Frequently	5 Very Often	6 Almost Always	7 Always
1	I receive the information needed to help me understand the performance of our organization							
2	I share information with others to help them understand the performance of our organization							
3	We demonstrate trust in people by sharing sensitive information about organization performance							
4	When I need information about our organization's performance, it is readily available for me to access							
5	When mistakes are made, we focus on correcting the problem not on who to blame							
6	When mistakes are made, we try to learn from the mistakes							

7	People in our organization get information about the organization's performance in a timely fashion									
8	We share information about organizational performance so that people can act responsibly to improve performance									
9	We share information in ways that break down traditional hierarchical thinking									
10	We get information into the hands of frontline people so they can make responsible decisions									

Section 5

Following questions are meant only for analysis purposes (Answer by writing or circle whichever is required):

1. Your age _____ years

2. Your sex (please tick one)
   __ 1. Male
   __ 2. Female

3. Your cultural background (Please tick one)
   __ 1. Malay   __ 3. Indian
   __ 2. Chinese   __ 4. Others (please specify) _____

4. How does your present job/position fit into the categories of staff? (Please tick one)
   __ 1. Middle level of management
   __ 2. Lower level of management
   __ 3. Other (please specify)

5   What is your educational level?
    __ 1. High school or below
    __ 2. Diploma
    __ 3. Degree or professional qualifications
    __ 4. Postgraduate

6   Your designation/position _____

7   What is your gross monthly salary?
    __ 1. Less than RM 1,500
    __ 2. Between RM 1,501 and RM 3,000
    __ 3. Between RM 3,001 and RM 5,000
    __ 4. Between RM 5,001 and RM 6,000
    __ 5. More than RM 6,000

8   Your company is (Please tick one)
    __ 1. Locally owned company   __ 3. Europe-based company
    __ 2. US-based company   __ 4. Others (please specify)

9   Is your organization a financial institution?
    __ 1. Yes
    __ 2. No

Thank you for your invaluable participation in this academic research!

APPENDIX B
SPSS Outputs

Frequencies

Statistics

		GENDER	Marital Status	Education
N	Valid	203	199	197
	Missing	3	7	9

Frequency Table

GENDER

		Frequency	Percent	Valid Percent	Cumulative Percent
Valid	Male	116	56.3	57.1	57.1
	Female	87	42.2	42.9	100.0
	Total	203	98.5	100.0	
Missing	System	3	1.5		
Total		206	100.0		

Marital Status

		Frequency	Percent	Valid Percent	Cumulative Percent
Valid	Married	88	42.7	44.2	44.2
	Single	101	49.0	50.8	95.0
	Divorced	8	3.9	4.0	99.0
	Widowed	2	1.0	1.0	100.0
	Total	199	96.6	100.0	
Missing	System	7	3.4		
Total		206	100.0		

Education

		Frequency	Percent	Valid Percent	Cumulative Percent
Valid	High School	84	40.8	42.6	42.6
	Diploma	68	33.0	34.5	77.2
	Bachelor degree	40	19.4	20.3	97.5
	Post-graduate	5	2.4	2.5	100.0
	Total	197	95.6	100.0	
Missing	System	9	4.4		
Total		206	100.0		

Descriptive

Descriptive Statistics

	N	Minimum	Maximum	Mean	Std. Deviation
Career Advancement & Opportunity	206	1.45	4.55	2.8373	.6711
Job Satisfaction	206	.30	4.70	3.2556	.6922
Organisation Commitment	206	.00	6.67	4.3575	1.1500
Organisation Empowerment & Trust	206	.00	5.00	3.5083	.9322
Valid N (listwise)	206				

Reliability Test for Career Advancement & Opportunity

* * * Method 1 (space saver) will be used for this analysis * * *

R E L I A B I L I T Y   A N A L Y S I S   -   S C A L E   (A L P H A)

		Mean	Std. Dev.	Cases
1.	AQ2	3.3010	.9301	206.0
2.	AQ3	3.2864	.9781	206.0
3.	AQ5 3	.1990	.9648	206.0
4.	AQ8	3.1990	.9129	206.0
5.	AQ10	3.2621	.9521	206.0
6.	AQ12	3.3252	.9192	206.0
7.	AQ13	3.3495	.9547	206.0
8.	AQ17	4.4563	1.6720	206.0
9.	AQ18	4.4223	1.4147	206.0
10.	AQ19	4.3641	1.5581	206.0
11.	AQ30	3.5680	1.2466	206.0

Reliability Coefficients

No. of cases = 206.0 No. of items = 11

Alpha = .8888

Reliability Test for Job Satisfaction

* * * Method 1 (space saver) will be used for this analysis * * *

RELIABILITY ANALYSIS - SCALE (ALPHA)

		Mean	Std. Dev.	Cases
1.	BQ1	3.5928	1.1217	194.0
2.	BQ2	3.5464	1.1873	194.0
3.	BQ3	3.4381	1.2545	194.0
4.	BQ4	3.4124	1.1894	194.0
5.	BQ5	3.5206	1.1881	194.0
6.	BQ6	3.5876	1.1718	194.0
7.	BQ7	3.6392	1.0839	194.0
8.	BQ8	3.6237	1.1596	194.0
9.	BQ9	1.4124	.4935	194.0
10.	BQ10	1.6186	.6183	194.0
11.	BQ11	1.4278	.4960	194.0
12.	BQ12	3.4639	3.0166	194.0
13.	BQ13	3.3299	.9299	194.0
14.	BQ14	3.3196	1.0436	194.0
15.	BQ15	3.3608	.9461	194.0
16.	BQ16	3.4639	3.0166	194.0
17.	BQ17	3.3299	.9299	194.0
18.	BQ18	3.3196	1.0436	194.0
19.	BQ19	3.3608	.9461	194.0
20.	BQ20	3.3814	.9651	194.0

Reliability Coefficients

No. of cases = 194.0   No. of items = 20

Alpha = .8355

Reliability Test for Organizational Commitment

* * * Method 1 (space saver) will be used for this analysis * * *

RELIABILITY ANALYSIS - SCALE (ALPHA)

		Mean	Std. Dev.	Cases
1.	CQ1	4.0000	1.3356	186.0
2.	CQ2	4.4247	1.2849	186.0
3.	CQ3	4.2688	1.3528	186.0
4.	CQ4	4.5215	1.3880	186.0
5.	CQ5	4.3333	1.3503	186.0
6.	CQ6	4.3333	1.4507	186.0
7.	CQ7	4.3656	1.3134	186.0
8.	CQ8	4.3065	1.3824	186.0
9.	CQ9	4.2903	1.3722	186.0
10.	CQ10	4.2849	1.2344	186.0
11.	CQ11	4.3118	1.3515	186.0
12.	CQ12	4.2258	1.4152	186.0
13.	CQ13	4.4570	1.3031	186.0
14.	CQ14	4.5108	3.3808	186.0
15.	CQ15	4.2151	1.3624	186.0

Reliability Coefficients

No. of cases = 186.0   No. of items = 15

Alpha = .9316

Reliability Test for Organizational Empowerment & Trust

* * * Method 1 (space saver) will be used for this analysis * * *

RELIABILITY ANALYSIS - SCALE (ALPHA)

		Mean	Std Dev	Cases
1.	DQ1	3.6422	1.3110	204.0
2.	DQ2	3.9559	2.4939	204.0
3.	DQ3	3.8137	1.2455	204.0
4.	DQ4	3.8922	1.3530	204.0
5.	DQ5	3.6127	1.4493	204.0
6.	DQ6	3.7157	1.3601	204.0
7.	DQ7	3.8971	3.1095	204.0
8.	DQ8	3.7402	1.2696	204.0
9.	DQ9	3.7647	1.2171	204.0
10.	DQ10	3.7941	1.2464	204.0

Reliability Coefficients

No. of cases = 204.0 No. of items = 10

Alpha = .8688

Partial Correlation

-—P A R T I A L C O R R E L A T I O N C O E F F I C I E N T S—-

Controlling for . . . GENDER MSTATUS

	CAO	JOBSAT	OC	OET
CAO	1.0000	-.6989	-.7172	-.7075
	(0)	(195)	(195)	(195)
	$p = .000$	$p = .000$	$p = .000$	$p = .000$
JOBSAT	-.6989	1.0000	.7499	.6112
	(195)	(0)	(195)	(195)
	$p = .000$	$p = .$	$p = .000$	$p = .000$
OC	-.7172	.7499	1.0000	.7163
	(195)	(195)	(0)	(195)
	$p = .000$	$p = .000$	$p = .$	$p = .000$
OET	-.7075	.6112	.7163	1.0000
	(195)	(195)	(195)	(0)
	$p = .000$	$p = .000$	$p = .000$	$p = .$

(Coefficient / (df) / one-tailed significance)

"." is printed if a coefficient cannot be computed

T-Test

Group Statistics

	AGE	N	Mean	Std. Deviation	Std. Error Mean
Career Advancement & Opportunity	>= 35.00	67	2.3615	.5129	6.266E-02
	< 35.00	137	3.0729	.6165	5.267E-02
Job Satisfaction	>= 35.00	67	3.7657	.5782	7.064E-02
	< 35.00	137	3.0204	.5519	4.715E-02
Organisation Commitment	>= 35.00	67	5.3055	.7922	9.679E-02
	< 35.00	137	3.9205	.9541	8.152E-02
Organisation Empowerment & Trust	>= 35.00	67	4.1403	.6147	7.510E-02
	< 35.00	137	3.2248	.8708	7.440E-02

Independent Samples Test

		Levene's Test for Equality of Variances		t-test for Equality of Means					95% Confidence Interval of the Difference	
		F	Sig.	t	df	Sig. (2-tailed)	Mean Difference	Std. Error Difference	Lower	Upper
Career Advancement & Opportunity	Equal variances assumed	8.732	.003	-8.162	202	.000	-.7114	8.716E-02	-.8833	-.5396
	Equal variances not assumed			-8.691	154.727	.000	-.7114	8.185E-02	-.8731	-.5497
Job Satisfaction	Equal variances assumed	1.012	.316	8.916	202	.000	.7452	8.358E-02	.5804	.9100
	Equal variances not assumed			8.774	125.799	.000	.7452	8.493E-02	.5772	.9133
Organisation Commitment	Equal variances assumed	3.063	.082	10.272	202	.000	1.3850	.1348	1.1192	1.6509
	Equal variances not assumed			10.945	154.995	.000	1.3850	.1265	1.1350	1.6350
Organisation Empowerment & Trust	Equal variances assumed	10.511	.001	7.712	202	.000	.9155	.1187	.6814	1.1495
	Equal variances not assumed			8.660	176.579	.000	.9155	.1057	.7069	1.1241

T-Test

Group Statistics

	GENDER	N	Mean	Std. Deviation	Std. Error Mean
Career Advancement & Opportunity	Male	116	2.8566	.7326	6.802E-02
	Female	87	2.8175	.5912	6.338E-02
Job Satisfaction	Male	116	3.2707	.6860	6.369E-02
	Female	87	3.2684	.6409	6.871E-02
Organisation Commitment	Male	116	4.3614	1.2058	.1120
	Female	87	4.3846	.9862	.1057
Organisation Empowerment & Trust	Male	116	3.5759	.9338	8.670E-02
	Female	87	3.4724	.8634	9.257E-02

Independent Samples Test

		Levene's Test for Equality of Variances		t-test for Equality of Means					95% Confidence Interval of the Difference	
		F	Sig.	t	df	Sig. (2-tailed)	Mean Difference	Std. Error Difference	Lower	Upper
Career Advancement & Opportunity	Equal variances assumed	6.313	.013	.408	201	.684	3.908E-02	9.584E-02	-.1499	.2281
	Equal variances not assumed			.420	199.889	.675	3.908E-02	9.297E-02	-.1443	.2224
Job Satisfaction	Equal variances assumed	.556	.457	.024	201	.981	2.299E-03	9.461E-02	-.1843	.1889
	Equal variances not assumed			.025	191.541	.980	2.299E-03	9.369E-02	-.1825	.1871
Organisation Commitment	Equal variances assumed	4.883	.028	-.147	201	.884	-2.322E-02	.1584	-.3356	.2892
	Equal variances not assumed			-.151	199.455	.880	-2.322E-02	.1540	-.3269	.2804
Organisation Empowerment & Trust	Equal variances assumed	1.109	.294	.807	201	.421	.1034	.1283	-.1495	.3564
	Equal variances not assumed			.816	192.361	.416	.1034	.1268	-.1467	.3536

T-Test

Group Statistics

	Marital Status	N	Mean	Std. Deviation	Std. Error Mean
Career Advancement & Opportunity	Married	88	2.5006	.5035	5.367E-02
	Single	101	3.1205	.6822	6.788E-02
Job Satisfaction	Married	88	3.5676	.6058	6.458E-02
	Single	101	2.9906	.5929	5.900E-02
Organisation Commitment	Married	88	4.9947	.9019	9.615E-02
	Single	101	3.7545	.9753	9.705E-02
Organisation Empowerment & Trust	Married	88	3.9659	.7073	7.539E-02
	Single	101	3.2000	.8993	8.949E-02

Independent Samples Test

		Levene's Test for Equality of Variances		t-test for Equality of Means					95% Confidence Interval of the Difference	
		F	Sig.	t	df	Sig. (2-tailed)	Mean Difference	Std. Error Difference	Lower	Upper
Career Advancement & Opportunity	Equal variances assumed	13.130	.000	-7.019	187	.000	-.6199	8.832E-02	-.7942	-.4457
	Equal variances not assumed			-7.164	182.243	.000	-.6199	8.664E-02	-.7907	-.4492
Job Satisfaction	Equal variances assumed	.287	.593	6.607	187	.000	.5770	8.734E-02	.4047	.7493
	Equal variances not assumed			6.597	182.327	.000	.5770	8.747E-02	.4044	.7496
Organisation Commitment	Equal variances assumed	.477	.491	9.030	187	.000	1.2402	.1373	.9693	1.5112
	Equal variances not assumed			9.078	186.321	.000	1.2402	.1366	.9707	1.5097
Organisation Empowerment & Trust	Equal variances assumed	3.680	.057	6.440	187	.000	.7659	.1189	.5313	1.0005
	Equal variances not assumed			6.546	185.132	.000	.7659	.1170	.5351	.9968

T-Test

Group Statistics

	Education	N	Mean	Std. Deviation	Std. Error Mean
Career Advancement & Opportunity	>= 2.50	45	2.4704	.5905	8.803E-02
	< 2.50	152	2.9507	.6671	5.411E-02
Job Satisfaction	>= 2.50	45	3.6244	.5331	7.947E-02
	< 2.50	152	3.1599	.6726	5.455E-02
Organisation Commitment	>= 2.50	45	4.8269	1.1148	.1662
	< 2.50	152	4.2230	1.0928	8.863E-02
Organisation Empowerment & Trust	>= 2.50	45	3.9289	.8777	.1308
	< 2.50	152	3.4237	.8673	7.035E-02

Independent Samples Test

		Levene's Test for Equality of Variances		t-test for Equality of Means					95% Confidence Interval of the Difference	
		F	Sig.	t	df	Sig. (2-tailed)	Mean Difference	Std. Error Difference	Lower	Upper
Career Advancement & Opportunity	Equal variances assumed	3.760	.054	-4.349	195	.000	-.4802	.1104	-.6980	-.2624
	Equal variances not assumed			-4.647	80.196	.000	-.4802	.1033	-.6858	-.2746
Job Satisfaction	Equal variances assumed	3.964	.048	4.252	195	.000	.4646	.1092	.2491	.6800
	Equal variances not assumed			4.820	89.456	.000	.4646	9.639E-02	.2731	.6561
Organisation Commitment	Equal variances assumed	1.525	.218	3.241	195	.001	.6039	.1863	.2364	.9713
	Equal variances not assumed			3.206	70.922	.002	.6039	.1883	.2283	.9794
Organisation Empowerment & Trust	Equal variances assumed	.321	.572	3.423	195	.001	.5052	.1476	.2141	.7963
	Equal variances not assumed			3.401	71.383	.001	.5052	.1485	.2090	.8014

One-Way ANOVA

Descriptives

		N	Mean	Std. Deviation	Std. Error	95% Confidence Interval for Mean		Minimum	Maximum
						Lower Bound	Upper Bound		
Career Advancement & Opportunity	Male	116	2.8566	.7326	6.802E-02	2.7218	2.9913	1.45	4.55
	Female	87	2.8175	.5912	6.338E-02	2.6915	2.9435	1.45	4.00
	Total	203	2.8398	.6743	4.733E-02	2.7465	2.9331	1.45	4.55
Job Satisfaction	Male	116	3.2707	.6860	6.369E-02	3.1445	3.3969	1.60	4.55
	Female	87	3.2684	.6409	6.871E-02	3.1318	3.4050	2.00	4.70
	Total	203	3.2697	.6654	4.670E-02	3.1776	3.3618	1.60	4.70
Organisation Commitment	Male	116	4.3614	1.2058	.1120	4.1396	4.5831	1.33	6.67
	Female	87	4.3846	.9862	.1057	4.1744	4.5948	2.47	6.20
	Total	203	4.3713	1.1144	7.822E-02	4.2171	4.5256	1.33	6.67
Organisation Empowerment & Trust	Male	116	3.5759	.9338	8.670E-02	3.4041	3.7476	1.00	5.00
	Female	87	3.4724	.8634	9.257E-02	3.2884	3.6564	1.00	5.00
	Total	203	3.5315	.9036	6.342E-02	3.4065	3.6566	1.00	5.00

ANOVA

		Sum of Squares	df	Mean Square	F	Sig.
Career Advancement & Opportunity	Between Groups	7.593E-02	1	7.593E-02	.166	.684
	Within Groups	91.780	201	.457		
	Total	91.856	202			
Job Satisfaction	Between Groups	2.627E-04	1	2.627E-04	.001	.981
	Within Groups	89.441	201	.445		
	Total	89.441	202			
Organisation Commitment	Between Groups	2.680E-02	1	2.680E-02	.021	.884
	Within Groups	250.836	201	1.248		
	Total	250.863	202			
Organisation Empowerment & Trust	Between Groups	.532	1	.532	.651	.421
	Within Groups	164.386	201	.818		
	Total	164.918	202			

One-Way ANOVA

Descriptives

		N	Mean	Std. Deviation	Std. Error	95% Confidence Interval for Mean		Minimum	Maximum
						Lower Bound	Upper Bound		
Career Advancement & Opportunity	Married	88	2.5006	.5035	5.367E-02	2.3939	2.6072	1.45	4.00
	Single	101	3.1205	.6822	6.788E-02	2.9858	3.2552	1.73	4.55
	Divorced	8	2.7375	.6160	.2178	2.2225	3.2525	1.91	3.55
	Widowed	2	3.0450	.3182	.2250	.1861	5.9039	2.82	3.27
	Total	199	2.8302	.6726	4.768E-02	2.7362	2.9242	1.45	4.55
Job Satisfaction	Married	88	3.5676	.6058	6.458E-02	3.4393	3.6960	2.00	4.70
	Single	101	2.9906	.5929	5.900E-02	2.8735	3.1076	1.60	4.55
	Divorced	8	3.6500	.7982	.2822	2.9827	4.3173	2.10	4.45
	Widowed	2	3.5000	7.071E-02	5.000E-02	2.8647	4.1353	3.45	3.55
	Total	199	3.2774	.6685	4.739E-02	3.1839	3.3708	1.60	4.70
Organisation Commitment	Married	88	4.9947	.9019	9.615E-02	4.8036	5.1858	2.80	6.67
	Single	101	3.7545	.9753	9.705E-02	3.5619	3.9470	1.33	6.20
	Divorced	8	5.3062	.6686	.2328	4.7557	5.8568	4.13	6.13
	Widowed	2	4.1000	4.243E-02	3.000E-02	3.7188	4.4812	4.07	4.13
	Total	199	4.3687	1.1207	7.945E-02	4.2121	4.5254	1.33	6.67
Organisation Empowerment & Trust	Married	88	3.9659	.7073	7.539E-02	3.8161	4.1158	2.00	5.00
	Single	101	3.2000	.8993	8.949E-02	3.0225	3.3775	1.00	4.90
	Divorced	8	3.3875	.7699	.2722	2.7439	4.0311	2.20	4.40
	Widowed	2	3.2500	7.071E-02	5.000E-02	2.6147	3.8853	3.20	3.30
	Total	199	3.5467	.8891	6.303E-02	3.4224	3.6710	1.00	5.00

ANOVA

		Sum of Squares	df	Mean Square	F	Sig.
Career Advancement & Opportunity	Between Groups	18.234	3	6.078	16.611	.000
	Within Groups	71.352	195	.366		
	Total	89.586	198			
Job Satisfaction	Between Groups	16.929	3	5.643	15.380	.000
	Within Groups	71.549	195	.367		
	Total	88.478	198			
Organisation Commitment	Between Groups	79.764	3	26.588	30.691	.000
	Within Groups	168.932	195	.866		
	Total	248.696	198			
Organisation Empowerment & Trust	Between Groups	27.984	3	9.328	14.150	.000
	Within Groups	128.551	195	.659		
	Total	156.535	198			

One-Way ANOVA

Descriptives

		N	Mean	Std. Deviation	Std. Error	95% Confidence Interval for Mean		Minimum	Maximum
						Lower Bound	Upper Bound		
Career Advancement & Opportunity	High School	84	3.2117	.6175	6.738E-02	3.0777	3.3457	1.45	4.55
	Diploma	68	2.6282	.5828	7.068E-02	2.4872	2.7693	1.55	4.27
	Bachelor degree	40	2.5110	.6058	9.578E-02	2.3173	2.7047	1.45	4.09
	Post-graduate	5	2.1460	.3313	.1481	1.7347	2.5573	1.73	2.55
	Total	197	2.8410	.6797	4.843E-02	2.7455	2.9365	1.45	4.55
Job Satisfaction	High School	84	2.9077	.6369	6.949E-02	2.7695	3.0460	1.60	4.55
	Diploma	68	3.4713	.5821	7.059E-02	3.3304	3.6122	2.35	4.70
	Bachelor degree	40	3.5788	.5134	8.118E-02	3.4146	3.7429	2.50	4.55
	Post-graduate	5	3.9900	.6066	.2713	3.2368	4.7432	3.10	4.50
	Total	197	3.2660	.6712	4.782E-02	3.1717	3.3603	1.60	4.70
Organisation Commitment	High School	84	3.7854	.9722	.1061	3.5744	3.9963	1.80	6.20
	Diploma	68	4.7637	.9917	.1203	4.5236	5.0037	2.40	6.33
	Bachelor degree	40	4.7520	1.1394	.1802	4.3876	5.1164	1.33	6.67
	Post-graduate	5	5.4260	.7119	.3184	4.5420	6.3100	4.53	6.13
	Total	197	4.3610	1.1241	8.009E-02	4.2030	4.5189	1.33	6.67
Organisation Empowerment & Trust	High School	84	2.9738	.7064	7.708E-02	2.8205	3.1271	1.20	4.70
	Diploma	68	3.9794	.7142	8.660E-02	3.8065	4.1523	2.20	5.00
	Bachelor degree	40	3.9850	.8625	.1364	3.7092	4.2608	1.00	5.00
	Post-graduate	5	3.4800	.9680	.4329	2.2781	4.6819	2.40	4.40
	Total	197	3.5391	.8931	6.363E-02	3.4136	3.6646	1.00	5.00

ANOVA

		Sum of Squares	df	Mean Square	F	Sig.
Career Advancement & Opportunity	Between Groups	21.390	3	7.130	19.897	.000
	Within Groups	69.163	193	.358		
	Total	90.554	196			
Job Satisfaction	Between Groups	20.182	3	6.727	19.060	.000
	Within Groups	68.120	193	.353		
	Total	88.302	196			
Organisation Commitment	Between Groups	50.647	3	16.882	16.539	.000
	Within Groups	197.006	193	1.021		
	Total	247.653	196			
Organisation Empowerment & Trust	Between Groups	47.996	3	15.999	28.497	.000
	Within Groups	108.353	193	.561		
	Total	156.349	196			

One-Way ANOVA

Descriptives

		N	Mean	Std. Deviation	Std. Error	95% Confidence Interval for Mean		Minimum	Maximum
						Lower Bound	Upper Bound		
Career Advancement & Opportunity	Executive	113	2.5321	.5252	4.940E-02	2.4342	2.6300	1.45	4.27
	Non-executive	84	3.2573	.6334	6.911E-02	3.1198	3.3947	1.45	4.55
	Total	197	2.8413	.6758	4.815E-02	2.7464	2.9363	1.45	4.55
Job Satisfaction	Executive	113	3.5283	.5611	5.279E-02	3.4237	3.6329	2.40	4.70
	Non-executive	84	2.9268	.6467	7.057E-02	2.7864	3.0671	1.60	4.50
	Total	197	3.2718	.6678	4.758E-02	3.1780	3.3657	1.60	4.70
Organisation Commitment	Executive	113	4.8414	1.0019	9.425E-02	4.6547	5.0282	1.33	6.67
	Non-executive	84	3.7575	.9589	.1046	3.5494	3.9656	1.80	6.20
	Total	197	4.3792	1.1188	7.971E-02	4.2220	4.5364	1.33	6.67
Organisation Empowerment & Trust	Executive	113	4.0159	.7464	7.021E-02	3.8768	4.1550	1.00	5.00
	Non-executive	84	2.9214	.6624	7.228E-02	2.7777	3.0652	1.20	4.70
	Total	197	3.5492	.8937	6.367E-02	3.4237	3.6748	1.00	5.00

ANOVA

		Sum of Squares	df	Mean Square	F	Sig.
Career Advancement & Opportunity	Between Groups	25.336	1	25.336	76.970	.000
	Within Groups	64.187	195	.329		
	Total	89.522	196			
Job Satisfaction	Between Groups	17.435	1	17.435	48.580	.000
	Within Groups	69.982	195	.359		
	Total	87.416	196			
Organisation Commitment	Between Groups	56.609	1	56.609	58.488	.000
	Within Groups	188.736	195	.968		
	Total	245.344	196			
Organisation Empowerment & Trust	Between Groups	57.720	1	57.720	113.906	.000
	Within Groups	98.813	195	.507		
	Total	156.532	196			

ABOUT THE AUTHOR

Kelechikwu Emmanuel, Oguejiofor

Is a Nigerian citizen whom had the distinct privilege of studying along the world best faculties "Nottingham Business School". Even as African their most envied career paths are "Lawyers, Medical Doctors and Engineers. However, regardless of parental pressure and projected justifications. Kelechikwu was convinced that globalization has given birth to constructive weapons to fight inefficiencies and as such pursued a career path in International Business from Nottingham Business School and graduated with "First class Honours". Kelechikwu has received commendable merit accolades; which are partial scholarship to pursue MBA, University of Derby, Membership grade of Chartered Management Institute and Membership of Academy of International Business. Kelechikwu is also a co founder of an "International consultancy company"

Finally as acknowledged Kelechikwu ultimately believes that despite barriers and inefficiency "Africa can still be positioned for Global Excellence" and this is observed as his earnest source of inspiration.

Advice: For business Stakeholders whom tactically manipulate human capital for profit maximization by profiteering the escape gloating or using status quo. This empirical finding is Not for You!

"Profit maximization means different things for various business stakeholders especially with globalization, intense competition and the global financial crisis. The said business stakeholders (i.e. Entrepreneurs, Business leaders, Managers, Investors and many more) are faced with much dilemma in marking those critical decisions that deems business competiveness. The quick fix model such as Downsizing, Retrenchment, Layoffs and many more are always emulated due to the phenomenal tendency to cut cost and these "short term fix "comes with intense disadvantage to the overall long term sustainable competiveness of such business. Thus, this empirical findings proposes "An art to master long term sustainable business competiveness' A model that utilize organizational commitment as a key ingredient to enhance productivity and turnover rather than the nowadays acceptable quick fix"

—Kelechikwu Emmanuel, Oguejiofor
Author

Kelechikwu Emmanuel, Oguejiofor
International consultant,
Business Researcher @ Derbyshire Business School

www.ingramcontent.com/pod-product-compliance
Lightning Source LLC
Chambersburg PA
CBHW021953170526
45157CB00003B/979